LOUIE
IN SEASON

LOUIE
IN SEASON

by
Lou Carnesecca
with **Phil Pepe**

McGraw-Hill Publishing Company
New York St. Louis San Francisco Auckland Bogotá
Hamburg London Madrid Mexico Milan Montreal
New Delhi Panama Paris São Paulo Singapore
Sydney Tokyo Toronto

1 2 3 4 5 6 7 8 9 DOC DOC 8 9 2 1 0 9 8

ISBN 0-07-010131-0

LIBRARY OF CONGRESS CATALOGING-IN-PUBLICATION DATA

Carnesecca, Lou.
  LOUIE: in season.

  1. Carnesecca, Lou.   2. Coaches—United States—
Biography.   3. St. John's University (New York, N.Y.)—
Basketball.   I. Pepe, Phil.   II. Title.
GV884.C35A3   1988   796.32'3'0924 [B]   88-23036
ISBN 0-07-010131-0

Book design by Mark Bergeron

This book is dedicated most lovingly to
my wife, Mary, for her untiring patience, her
understanding, and for always being there

Contents

Foreword

A couple of years ago, I told Lou Carnesecca he was a natural for elected office.

He became indignant. "Are you saying I'm a liar, Mario?"

What I meant was that the skills he developed over forty years of coaching could be successfully applied to another game—the game of politics.

The first thing good politicians learn is to control their temper. Louie had a reputation for competitive ferocity when, on graduation, he switched from being a player to assistant baseball coach at St. John's.

Yet when I met him soon after the switch, in 1950, he had already made it his business to mellow. Head coach Frank McGuire allowed Louie to dole out compliments while he, Frank, attended to discipline. When McGuire decided that his center fielder Cuomo who wanted to play no other position, would better serve the team as a catcher, Louie did what any smart politician would do: He got out of the line of fire and kept his mouth shut.

I can still see Louie's look of dismay as I suggested to the respected Mr. McGuire what he could do with the catcher's mitt, and he told me where I could take my fielder's glove—to some other team. Louie was back-pedaling faster and faster away from the scene, as our voices rose. Louie has always understood when to press and when to fall back.

Louie relates to basketball players as he does to members of his own family—on the basis of mutual respect. His approach can be summed up this way: "Here is my coaching philosophy; it is broad enough to let you gifted individuals play your game but to do so within the team concept."

In recent years, the system accommodated the unorthodox, serpentine moves of Walter Berry, the heady play of the sharpshooting Chris Mullin and the all-around floor generalship of Mark Jackson. It permitted the three of them to attain stardom in college and then in the NBA.

Louie raises the level of players of lesser ability by making them believe *he* believes they can rise to any challenge. Just as important, he imparts that faith to everyone who follows St. John's basketball. More is expected of Louie's teams because of his confidence in them. Year in, year out, Carnesecca's Redmen find a way to match even the most inflated expectations.

It's not only his players whom Louie makes better; it's everybody he knows. When friends cause him pain, as McGuire and I did long ago, Louie's memory absolves the culprits, transforms encounters like ours into displays of admirable spirit: You should hear Louie tell the story.

Louie has refined the skill of using elegant evasions and hyperbole to make people feel good about themselves. He does it naturally, credibly as an inspirational chief executive should.

I only wish I were half as good—and half as successful—as my favorite coach and one of my favorite people, Louis Carnesecca.

Governor Mario M. Cuomo

Preface

As a student, I never knew Lou Carnesecca at St. John's, having arrived on campus two years after he left. I met him a few years later, after I had embarked on a career as a sportswriter with the now-defunct *New York World Telegram & Sun*. I was a rookie reporter assigned to cover local high school sports; Carnesecca was, by then, a veteran coach of four years at St. Ann's Academy. In my new world, he was an important figure, having won two city Catholic schools championships in basketball. As such, he was a vital source for many of the stories I wrote for my newspaper.

I remember vividly how patient, cooperative, and accessible he was to a young reporter in those days. He was understanding of my needs and he was available to help me do my job.

Before long, we both moved on: Lou became assistant coach at St. John's; I began covering college sports. Again, he was a great aid in helping me do my job—always available, always ready with an encouraging word.

By the 1960s, I had moved on to other assignments—major league baseball, boxing, a daily sports column—and our paths did not cross quite as often as before. However, I followed his career closely as an interested observer and as a St. John's alumnus, and I took great vicarious pride in his success. Our meetings, though less frequent, were always pleasant, cordial, and fun. When the idea of collaborating with "Looie" on his autobiography was first presented to me, I eagerly looked forward to the opportunity of spending more time with him.

Observing a man from afar is one thing. Working closely with him is quite another. The experience taught me to appreciate Lou Carnesecca on many different levels—as a man of great depth, compassion, understanding, and warmth.

I learned that Lou Carnesecca does not come by his success accidentally. The trademarks of his success are hard work, dedication, and an abiding concern for his co-workers, his players, and his colleagues as well as a deep love for his chosen profession. Most important, Lou Carnesecca wears his success well—without, as he likes to say, "blowing his own bugle."

Lou Carnesecca's most enduring quality has been his enduring quality. He is remarkable for his longevity in a most competitive and often cut-throat business, almost 40 years coaching in the toughest, most cynical, most demanding of arenas—New York City. His friends and fans are legion. His enemies, to my knowledge, are nonexistent.

His record speaks for itself—among active coaches he is in the top 10 in number of victories; he has had more post-season appearances than any active coach; as a coach on three levels (high school, college and pro) he had a post-season appearance in every year; he was coach of two consecutive John Wooden Award winners; and he was voted national coach of the year once and Coach of the Year in the Big East three times.

He never got the best players, but he made the players he did get better, and his teams are always competitive. He did all this with a sense of morality, a sense of loyalty, a sense of caring for his kids, without compromise and without "taking home the chandeliers," to borrow another of his favorite expressions.

Few men are as happy in their jobs and as content in their lives as Lou Carnesecca. Basketball is his life, his passion. He has a reverence for the game he has graced; he has a deep respect for his profession and for all those who share it with him. But, do not paint the man as one-dimensional. He has had time for other people and for other interests. Still, basketball remains the cornerstone of his life.

Through basketball he has gained a measure of fame and recognition, financial security, and the opportunity to broaden himself by traveling around the world. He has learned to appreciate the port wine of Portugal, the tango of Argentina, the flamenco of Spain, and the Neapolitan folk songs of his forebears. He enjoys a Puccini opera as well as a Cole Porter lyric sung by Frank Sinatra or Ella Fitzgerald. He digs Count Basie's "One O'Clock Jump," a Lionel Hampton solo on the vibes, or a Benny Goodman lick on the clarinet.

Lou Carnesecca is a man who takes his work seriously but not himself. He has learned to laugh at himself and at others who laugh with him. It is an endearing quality.

"I call him the absent-minded perfectionist," Katha Quinn, St. John's estimable Sports Information Director, told me. "When I ask him to pose for a picture with one of our taller players, he'll give me one of his professorial looks and say, 'Katha, you're making fun at my anatomical structure again.'"

I asked Katha for one favorite Louie story. This is what she offered:

"It was 1979 and we played in the Eastern Regionals down in Atlantic Coast Conference country. It was known as 'Black Sunday' because all the ACC teams lost on their home courts to teams from the East. We were coming back to New York before heading for the regional semifinals. The press had arranged with me that when we arrived at the airport in New York, we would hold the team back until the other passengers got off. Then we would disembark into a welcoming committee of reporters, TV cameras, cheerleaders, and fans.

"It was a big day for St. John's. The whole city was proud of what the team had done, so I arranged the whole thing. I told Coach and the ballplayers what to expect and that I would appreciate their cooperation. So, everybody gets off and then the team gets off. Cameras are clicking, reporters are interviewing players, and for some unknown reason, Coach Carnesecca gets turned around. Now, he's standing in front of a group of people, shaking hands, and telling the people, 'Thank you for coming to see us.'

"Twenty feet behind him, the band is playing and the cameras and cheerleaders are taking this all in. The group of people are looking at him with blank expressions on their faces, as if they had no idea what this little guy was babbling on about.

"It suddenly occurred to me. At about the same time we landed, a plane had arrived from Poland with visitors who had never been to this country before and could not speak a word of English. And Coach had gotten turned around and he was thanking a group of Polish visitors for coming to see him. They must have thought Americans were the most hospitable people in the world, or that this little guy was out of his mind.

"I rushed up to him, turned him around, and told him what he had done.

" 'You mean I thanked the wrong people?' he asked innocently."

That's Louie—innocent, ambassador to the world, and completely unpretentious. Watching him is a kick. Listening to him is an experience. Working with him has been a joy. I can only hope that I have captured him, the flavor of his language, his personality, his zest for life, and his love for his profession.

Many people helped in the preparation of this book and Lou and I wish to thank each of them: Governor Mario M. Cuomo; the Very Reverend Joseph T. Cahill, C.M.; Reverend Robert J. Rivard, C.M.; Reverend Walter T. Graham, C.M.; Reverend Joseph Dorr, C.M.; Jack Kaiser; Jack Gimmler; Dick Laskowski; Katha Quinn; Frank Racaniello; Bill Esposito; Connie Maffei; Tom Quinn; Bruce Levy; Basil Kane; Dr. Irwin Glick; Dr. Ralph Squitieri; Dean Henry Rossi; Marilyn Lauder; Bernie Beglane; Carmine Piacentini; Dave Tilzar; Bill McKeever; Dean Patrick Basilice; John Kresse; Marty Satalino; Brian Mahoney; Ron Rutledge; Al LoBalbo; the Vincentian Fathers; the faculty and staff at St. John's; high school, junior college, college and professional coaches everywhere; and the hundreds of young men who had the rare and rewarding experience of being one of "Louie's Boys" in his almost 40 years of coaching basketball.

Phil Pepe

Introduction

The basketball season hasn't even begun and already I'm in trouble again with my mouth. When will I ever learn? When I arrived at my office in St. John's Alumni Hall this morning, waiting for me was Katha Quinn, the extremely competent and affable director of sports information here at St. John's. Katha looks after me like a mother hen. She says I drive her crazy, that I have a clock that runs on Rome time, and that the most important tools of her trade are the pair of sneakers she needs to keep up with me.

Katha has been a tower of strength in helping me deal with the press, which I consider an important part of my job. This morning, from the strange and sheepish look on her face, I could tell I was in trouble again.

Katha said she had a letter from Dean Smith asking her to please tell Coach Carnesecca that his name is Dean, not Dean-o.

"Coach Smith said he would appreciate it if you would please call him Dean in the future," Katha said.

"All right," I said, absently. "Tell Dean-o that's fine with me. Everything is cool."

I like Dean Smith. And I respect him for the job he has done at the University of North Carolina. He has been one of the best, and most successful, college basketball coaches for years. But sometimes I get the feeling that he takes things a little too seriously. I once called him a name and he didn't talk to me for five years. I don't even remember what it was I called him, probably a four-letter word, but I didn't mean anything by it.

Whatever I called him, I'm sure I meant it affectionately. Where I come from—New York's East Side—that's what we did with our friends. That's the way we greeted each other. It's a sign of affection, not of disrespect or hostility, but Dean just didn't understand that.

I certainly didn't want to offend Dean. I try not to offend anyone, at least not on purpose. It's just that sometimes I say things that I think are harmless, with no disrespect or hostility intended, and they're taken the wrong way. I'm sorry when that happens. I feel badly about it. But I guess I'm too set in my ways to change the way I am.

Katha says the way I am is disorganized. She says that I walk to the beat of my own drummer, and he's usually off key; that I have my own way of doing things and nobody is going to change me after all these years. I have to admit she's right. She laughs at my filing system, for example. My telephone book is the same one I have used for decades. It's filled with scratches and corrections and notes that only I can understand. When somebody dies, for instance, I haven't the heart to remove his name and phone number from my book. I simply write "RIP" next to his name.

I can converse fairly fluently in Spanish and Italian, and I can get by in French. Katha likes to say I can speak every language except English.

Katha also enjoys telling people about overhearing me having a telephone conversation with my wife, Mary. We had arranged to have some carpenters come to the house to do some work and Mary called me all upset because the carpenters had not shown up on schedule. When she called them, they told her they were too busy and they wouldn't be able to get there for several days. I guess I must have become just as frustrated as Mary was because Katha says I blurted into the telephone, "For God's sake, Mary, who the hell is the carpenter you hired to do this work, Joseph of Nazareth?"

I have to admit that I am a little disorganized. I sometimes play the role of the absentminded professor, which amuses my friends. Once I attended the weekly basketball writers luncheon at Mamma Leone's restaurant in midtown Manhattan. The luncheon is over and I go to the parking lot to get my car.

"A blue Chevrolet," I tell the parking lot attendant, handing him my ticket.

He looks all around and he comes back and says there is no blue Chevrolet on the lot.

"What do you mean?" I said. "I know I drove my car here."

"I'm sorry, sir, there is no blue Chevrolet on the lot."

Now I figure my car was stolen, so I call the police to report a stolen car. Then I called Mary and told her she had to come to Mamma Leone's to pick me up.

"How can I pick you up?" she said. "You have my car."

"What do you mean I have your car?"

"Your car is being fixed," she said. "Don't you remember, you took my car this morning?"

Another time, I was in my office at St. John's and I had to go to my car to get something and I realized I had lost my keys. I called everybody in the office to join in the search for my keys. I figured they had to be there somewhere because I remember driving to work and I'm pretty sure I had my keys with me when I was driving.

That was nothing new to anybody. I lose my keys about three or four times a year. But we searched everywhere. No keys.

I appealed to my friend, Jack Gimmler, to help me find my keys. Jack, who is now Assistant Athletic Director and golf coach at St. John's, was our athletic trainer at the time. He also had been a much-decorated hero with the New York City Fire Department. I figured anybody who could pull people out of burning buildings, as Jack had done, would have no trouble finding a set of car keys.

Gimmler looked all around, but he couldn't find them, either. So he decided to give up the search and he offered to drive me home. I didn't have an extra set of keys because I had already lost my quota of three sets that year, so Gimmler drove me to the Chevrolet dealer to get another set of keys made up. It took about two days for them to get a new lock and a set of keys, so my car sat there in the parking lot at St. John's until the lock and keys were ready.

Finally, I pick up my keys and I get my car and go home. I walk in the door and Mary said she didn't feel like cooking that night and she suggests that I go get a pizza. I get in my car and pick up the pizza and while I'm driving home, some guy behind me is honking at me.

"HONK . . . HONK . . . HONK . . ." he's going. I'm in a lousy mood over losing my keys as it is and the more this guy honks, the more irritable I'm getting. We come to a red light and I stick my head out the window and I yell to the guy in the car behind me.

"What the hell are you honking at me for?"

"I'm sorry, sir," he said. "I just wanted to let you know that you left your keys in the trunk."

I really felt bad.

What I feel right now, at this stage of my life is a certain inner tranquility. I'm at peace with myself. I feel very fortunate to have worked for almost forty years at a job that I love, to have been associated with a game that I love. I still look forward to every season, every game. I still care.

There aren't many people who are fortunate enough to look forward to going to work every day; a lot of people look upon their jobs as drudgery. I have never felt that way about my job. Not one day in almost forty years. I consider myself one of the fortunate few.

I heard a story once that Tom Lasorda, the manager of the Los Angeles Dodgers, likes to tell at banquets.

"My wife once said, 'You know, Tom, sometimes I think you love baseball more than you love me.'

"I thought about that for a while," Lasorda said. "Then I said, 'Yeah, but I love you more than football and basketball.' "

That's the way I feel about basketball.

I have been privileged to have known and been associated with the greats of the game of basketball, the great coaches and the great players. I have traveled all over the world. I have met popes and governors and heads of state.

I also feel fortunate to have been on the sports scene in a tough and demanding sports city like New York for forty years. I don't know of any other sports figure who has been here longer with the exception of Wellington Mara of the football Giants, and he owns the team.

I have seen tremendous growth in the sport of basketball in my time. I watched the game come out of the small college gyms to the big arenas. I was there at the birth of the Big East conference, and I have witnessed it as it became one of the best, and I believe one of the strongest leagues in the country. I was against the idea in the beginning, but I was wrong. I was being selfish and shortsighted. The Big East has been a boon for eastern college basketball and for St. John's.

I have seen the NCAA tournament evolve into one of the most exciting, most compelling, most popular, and, yes, most profitable sporting events of its time. I have seen television help the game of college basketball grow beyond my wildest dreams and to have been a part of it has been a source of great satisfaction.

I have seen the down side, too. I lived through four point-shaving scandals. I watched the game almost destroyed only to pull itself up again and regain public favor, which I consider testimony to what a great game it really is. I have seen drugs enter the scene to where it is now our biggest problem, something that concerns me every day of my life. But I am confident we will survive this terrible scourge just as we survived the betting scandals.

I have had my differences with the NCAA, which I don't think has always made good decisions. But we are the NCAA, each member college and, overall, I think the organization has done a great job for college sports in general and college basketball in particular. But I think there is still room for changes. The organization has new, progressive leadership now that I believe is going to do the right thing and make those necessary changes that will move college sports ahead in the future.

I have seen the role of the player change dramatically with the rapid growth of the college game and it worries me that we are asking eighteen- and nineteen-year-old kids to conduct themselves like professionals; I worry that we're putting too much pressure on our kids and that we may be guilty of exploiting them.

I also have seen tremendous changes in the coaching profession. When I started, St. John's had only two coaches, a head coach and an assistant. The head coach often doubled as baseball coach and the assistant coach would coach the freshman basketball and freshman baseball teams. The head coach might arrive on campus in October and leave about March 15. Today, coaching is a full-time job and a year-round job. The head coach has become more of an administrator and organizer. He is a public relations man, a marketing man, and then he is a coach. He has as many as three or four full-time assistants who are in charge of recruiting, scouting, the whole cannoli.

I have had the experience of coaching in the professional ranks for three seasons with the Nets. I believe it was an experience that helped me a great deal. I got a cram course in three years that was the equivalent of ten years of college coaching. I learned how to deal with egos, how to handle diverse personalities, all of which I used when I returned for my second tour of duty here at St. John's.

If I have a philosophy of coaching, it's the philosophy of St. John's, something that has been handed down from Buck Freeman, Joe Lapchick, and Frank McGuire, who preceded me here. They were three of the greatest coaches the game has known, three of basketball's greatest minds, and each of them coached right here at St. John's. I feel privileged to have known each of them intimately, to have had the opportunity to learn from them, to work with them, and to work for them.

St. John's always has enjoyed a great reputation nationwide because of its basketball program and because of Buck Freeman, Joe Lapchick, and Frank McGuire. Mention St. John's and the first thing you think of is basketball. All over the country. All over the world. And that's because of those three great coaches—Freeman, Lapchick and McGuire—and because of Madison Square Garden, the most famous arena in the world.

I learned so much from all three of my predecessors. A couple of things, in particular, stay with me. They always will. I remember Lapchick—"the Big Indian," they used to call him—saying, "Don't go around blowing your own horn. Don't be a Harry James."

Joe hated the so-called geniuses of the game, the guys who thought they were more important than the players, that they were smarter than everybody else, that they, not the players, were responsible for the success of their teams. Joe hated phonies.

Buck Freeman was the same way. I once asked Buck, "If you had a measuring rod from 1 to 100, what do you think would be the percentage as far as the importance of personnel and coaching?"

Buck surprised me with his answer. He said personnel was worth 65–75 percent, coaching 15–20 percent.

"That's all we're worth?" I said, shocked at his answer and maybe a little disappointed, too.

"That's all," Buck repeated. "And don't forget the missing 5–20 percent. Luck."

That concept really hit home for me when I coached the Nets. One year we made the finals of the ABA playoffs with Rick Barry playing for us. The following year Barry was gone. Same coach, same plays, same concept, most of the same players, and we lost fifty games. So who was the most important person in our success the previous year, the coach or Rick Barry? I think the answer is obvious.

That's the St. John's philosophy handed down from generation to generation. (1) The players win. (2) Don't think you're a genius. If you take the credit and think you're so smart when you win, how smart are you when you lose?

At St. John's, we always have preached that you, as the coach, are not bigger than the school and you're not bigger than the players.

St. John's has won more basketball games than any college in the country with the exception of Kentucky, North Carolina, and Kansas. We have the third best winning percentage of all time and I'm proud to have had a part in that great tradition. I am also proud that I have coached more than 1,200 games in high school, college, and professional basketball and, thank the good Lord, I have never missed a game. I have won more than 800 games, or, more accurately, my players have won more than 800 games.

I am proud of my record, but I'm more proud of the players who have played for me through the years. I still stay in touch with most of them, all the way back to the players who played on my first team at St. Ann's Academy.

I am the son of immigrant parents who came to the United States from Italy and never even had a grammar school education. I never was good enough to make my college basketball team, yet I have had the privilege of coaching for almost forty years and of traveling all around the world and meeting such wonderful people. I am grateful for all that.

I have reached the finals of the National Invitation Tournament, won a few Holiday Festival championships, made it to the American Basketball Association finals and to the Final Four of the NCAA tournament. The one thing that has eluded me, I suppose, is that I never have won a national championship. It would be nice to win for myself, sure, but mostly for the university and for the kids. But I never have felt that would be the culmination of my career, the final point. The culmination has simply been coaching, doing what I have loved and being fortunate to have done it for so long. That's why at this stage of my career, after almost forty years in basketball, I am at peace with myself.

ONE

Tuscany to
New York

My roots go back to Pontremoli, a little mountain town in the Tuscany region of Italy. Mom and Pop both came from the same town. They knew each other in Italy but didn't get married until they came to the United States, first Mom, then Pop.

Tuscans are famous for four things. They love to eat, they love to drink, they love to gab, and they are the greatest cursers in the world. I qualify as a true son of Tuscany. I like my fettucine or rigatoni in light red sauce as much as the next guy. I love to talk. I'm not much for hard liquor, but I love my vino. And I must admit that my language, especially during a game, sometimes embarrasses the good Vincentian Fathers, who usually pretend not to hear me.

I try to watch my language, really I do. But sometimes I get so caught up in the game, I'm not even aware of what I'm saying. When I coached the Nets, I set the official ABA record. Barney Kremenko, the longtime New York sportswriter who was serving as our director of public relations, said he counted 147 curse words in a regular game (not 147 different words—I'm not that creative—I'm sure I repeated some a few times). Then we played overtime and I reeled off thirty-seven more. I never have come close to that at St. John's, but, remember, the pro game is forty-eight minutes long; the college game is only forty minutes.

Mom—her name is Adele—came to this country when she was twenty-one years old. She came alone, which had to be a frightening thing for a young girl who spoke no English. Her parents stayed in Italy, but her father saved up the money to send her to the United States. Times were bad in Italy back then. There was barely enough to eat, no money, no reason for optimism. Mom was sent to the United States for that corny, but true, old reason: to find a better life. Not necessarily gold in the streets, but greater opportunity.

Those who lived well in Italy stayed there. There was no reason to leave. People with status, with titles, with land, could live a very comfortable life. The others had very little choice; stay and suffer in poverty or go to the promising New World.

Mom was sent to a family friend here. The friend was going to take her in, help her get a job, and help her get acclimated to her new home.

I remember Mom telling me that when she arrived in the United States and the boat landed at Ellis Island, they discovered that a baby on board was sick with a communicable disease. As a precaution, they quarantined everyone on the boat for forty days and they poured kerosene on all the women and children, presumably to kill the disease.

The plan was for Mom to go to Pennsylvania, where she had relatives who would take her in and care for her. But a friend of the family picked her up at Ellis Island and Mom just stayed with the friend in New York. I don't think Mom even knew where she was. It was unbelievable how in those days people wound up where they did, often by mere accident or coincidence.

I wonder how my life would have changed if Mom had made it to Pennsylvania instead of New York. Would I have wound up coaching Villanova or St. Joseph's instead of St. John's? Or would I have become a farmer or a bricklayer?

It wasn't long after she arrived that Mom found work. She answered an ad in *Il Progresso*, the Italian language newspaper in New York. You might say Mom got her job through *Il Progresso*, to paraphrase another newspaper's advertisement. The ad offered a job to a young woman who spoke Italian. The job was a combination domestic and nanny for a rather well-to-do family in Harlem, a fancy neighborhood in the twenties and thirties.

The Ruggiero family lived in a big house on 115th Street in Upper Manhattan, Harlem. The Ruggieros had three children and the parents wanted a young woman to talk to them in Italian so that the kids would learn the language of their ancestors. The three kids grew up to be a doctor, a lawyer, and a funeral director, so Mom apparently did a pretty good job.

The Ruggieros were very good to her. They didn't treat her as a servant. They treated her as a member of the family. She ate with them, went on vacations with them, did everything with them. They were very kind to her.

Pop followed Mom here a few months later. He wanted to come to New York, but he had to go to California because his brother had gone there. He tried to jump the train but couldn't do it. So he went all the way to California, then turned around and came back to New York.

Of course, Pop was coming to New York to find Mom so they could get married. Shortly after he got here, they did get married. A few years later, in 1925, I was born to Alfred and Adele Carnesecca, their only child. They named me Luigi, after my paternal grandfather. The last name, Carnesecca, means "dried meat" in Italian, which turned out to be prophetic.

Pop's trade was stone masonry. His whole family were stone masons because they came from the mountains and that's where they learned their trade. Pop's father, his uncles, and his three brothers all were stone masons. But there was no stone masonry work here, so Pop became a brick layer. But he had problems. He didn't know the proper technique for laying bricks. He really was a stone mason who took pride in his artistry, but as a bricklayer, speed was of the essence. Pop wouldn't hurry because he wanted to do the job right, and the foreman would come to him and say, "Hey, goombah, you think you're building St. Peter's Basilica?"

There was very little work and Pop was too slow to catch on to the American way, so he decided to give up bricklaying and he opened a little grocery store on 102nd Street in East Harlem, which is where I spent the first eight years of my life.

We spoke only Italian at home when I was a kid. You had to speak Italian if you wanted to eat. I didn't start speaking English until I was six years old and I went to school, although there are some people who will tell you I still don't speak English.

The neighborhood where I grew up was a true melting pot—Italians, Jews, blacks, Hispanics, Czechs, Germans, Irish. Just about every ethnic group you can mention.

The neighborhood was tough. My big thing in those days was going to the movies, the Star Theater. My mother would take me to the movies three times a week, every Tuesday, Thursday, and Sunday. We'd go to the Italian theater and the films were all in Italian. That's without subtitles. People would bring their dinner with them to the movie, the spaghetti and the lasagna. You could smell the sauce and the garlic throughout the theater.

I remember one night coming home from the movies with my mother and almost getting caught in the cross fire of gun shots. Two families were shooting at each other. It seems some guy had been fooling around with another guy's girl friend. It turned out this guy liked to play, but he couldn't fly. They threw him off the roof and that started the gun battle between the two families. Luckily, the police came and broke it up before anybody was shot. That's how tough the neighborhood was.

Like most Tuscans, my father was a gregarious man. He was a wonderful man, full of fun and extremely generous. But he was no businessman. Mom had the business head in the family. Pop would give away the whole store if Mom didn't watch him. I'm afraid I'm a lot like Pop, outgoing and friendly, but not very good at business and very disorganized.

We lived in a poor neighborhood and times were tough, anyway, because of the Depression. People didn't have jobs and there was hardly enough money for food, so Pop would carry most of the people in the neighborhood on the books. People would come in for groceries and they didn't have the money to pay for them, so Pop would give them the groceries and put their names on a piece of paper and tell them they could pay him when they had the money. I'm sure he never collected everything he was owed, or he would lose the piece of paper and he would be out the money that was due him. Many days, he would take in as little as $11 gross.

As if that wasn't enough, Pop had a little room in the back of the store (we lived in an apartment upstairs, over the store) where he always kept a bottle of wine. Customers would come in and Pop would invite them into the back room for "un bichiere di vino," a glass of wine. Not only weren't they paying for the groceries, they were being entertained by the store owner.

Pop also had a table in the back room and every day, just about any time of day, you could go back there and there would be Pop and his friends playing a friendly little game of briscola, an Italian card game, and drinking their vino. A friend of Pop's would come in and order a pound of prosciutto and Pop would say, "Aspetta (wait), come on in the back and have a glass of wine first." And the guy would be there for hours. Pop loved to be with people. The more confusion, the more chaos, the happier he was.

When I was eight years old, Pop took seriously ill. The doctor came and examined him and his remedy was about the same as his remedy for just about any illness in those days.

"Alfredo," he said. "Go back to the old country. Go back to Italy and breathe the fresh air of the mountains and you will be as good as new in no time."

In our neighborhood, a doctor was like a god. He was admired and respected by everyone and whatever he said was taken as gospel. So Pop put the store up for sale, gathered up his belongings and every nickel we had, and off we went to the old country. We spent a little more than a year there. I even went to school in Italy, which is one of the reasons, I think, that I'm able to converse in Italian to this day. We might have stayed longer than a year. Who knows, we might have stayed there forever, but the economy was still bad and the political climate was filled with tension.

This was just before World War II broke out and Europe was not the place to be at a time like that. So Pop decided to leave Italy and we returned to the United States, back to New York. This time, however, instead of returning to East Harlem, we settled on the East Side, 62nd Street, between First and Second Avenues, where Pop opened up another grocery store.

Things did not exactly change very much in our new digs. Pop was no better businessman upon his return, no less gregarious or hospitable. He still carried people on the arm and he still entertained friends in his back room over coffee, a glass of vino, and a piece of cheese. But the economy had improved. The Depression was over, jobs were more plentiful and now people were paying their bills more readily, so our economic state did improve somewhat. Not that we were living in the lap of luxury, mind you, but we were comfortable. At least, there always was enough to eat.

Actually, Pop had two stores on 62nd Street, both between First and Second Avenues. The first one had to be closed when the city built the 59th Street Bridge. The city bought up all the property that stood where the bridge had been planned, but all Pop got from the city for the store was six hundred dollars. He moved down the street and opened another store, which turned out to be a better location.

As far back as I can remember, I always had to help out in the store, little chores like sweeping and stocking the shelves. I didn't like doing it very much because I would much rather be playing ball, but I recognized my obligation, even at a young age.

But, like most kids, I was mischievous at times and would like to have a little fun, play little games. One night, after Pop had closed the store for the day, he asked me to help him store a new stock of toilet tissue. I was about 10 or 11 at the time. So Pop climbed up on the ladder, and my job was to toss him the tissue, one roll at a time, and Pop would place it on the shelf.

For awhile, things went along very well. Then, I must have become bored, or I must have been in a particularly mischievous mood, because I decided to have some fun. Instead of throwing the rolls right into Pop's hand, I began to throw them to the left, then to the right, then a little farther away so that Pop would have to stretch out to reach them. A little farther, then a little farther. With each roll I tossed, Pop had to reach out a little more. Now he began to get annoyed.

"Louie," he said in a tone of warning.

But I was having too much fun to stop now and continued to throw the rolls away from him so he would have to stretch for them.

"LOUIE!"

Then, I went a little too far. I threw one that Pop had to reach out for and, sure enough, he lost his footing and he came tumbling down off the ladder.

"Bruto di disgraziato," he shouted.

At first I was scared at what I had done, until I realized Pop wasn't hurt, and I started laughing. Now Pop begins chasing me and I take off for dear life, out the store, up the stairs, heading for the apartment. Just as I get to the door of the apartment, Pop catches up to me. He grabs me and he starts taking his strap off and I figure I'm in for the beating of my life. But I still can't stop laughing.

And the next thing I know, Pop begins to laugh, too. We're rolling on the floor together, father and son, both of us laughing uncontrollably and Pop is hugging and kissing me.

The store and the neighborhood were just about Pop's entire life. At night, after he locked up, he would go across the street to a restaurant called "Il Vagobondo," where they had bocci courts, and he would play bocci with his cronies and drink more wine until one, two in the morning.

It was here, on the East Side of New York, that I began what was to be a lifelong love affair with sports, something that Pop never could understand. He thought sports were a waste of time and when he discovered that I would sneak out at every opportunity, with Mom's help, to indulge my new passion for sports in street games and on rock-strewn fields, he worried that I would never amount to anything.

Pop never appeared to be interested in spectator sports, although he was an avid fisherman and hunter until the day he died. It wasn't until he was in his seventies, and I was well into my coaching career at St. John's, that I learned he used to sneak into our games without ever telling me. I could have provided tickets to our games whenever he wanted them. Heaven knows, I have given out thousands of tickets in my time. But Pop would never ask. Instead, when St. John's was playing at Madison Square Garden, he would close the store early, jump into a cab, go to the Garden, buy a ticket and watch the game. Then he would be gone before I ever knew he was there. It wasn't until after he died, that a man named Emil Lusardi, the security director for the Garden, told me about all the times Pop would show up at the games. He'd find Emil, who would stash Pop in a seat where I couldn't see him, and Pop would tell Emil not to ever let on that he was there. Pop didn't want me to know he was at the games.

As I was growing up, Pop kept insisting that I had to go to school and become a doctor.

"Be a doctor," he used to say. "Be a somebody."

I guess it was typical of every Italian father that he wanted his son to become a doctor and play the accordion. And it was typical of my rebellious nature that I became a coach and played the clarinet. I really broke his horns.

Back in the United States, I indulged my passion for sports, often without Pop's knowledge or approval, and I fought the age-old battle of adolescence. It was in New York that I first met two women who would have a profound influence on my life.

One was Mary Chiesa, who would become my wife and the mother of our daughter, Enes. I met Mary when I was 13. We grew up together and just sort of started going out together. Mary's family came from the same region in Italy as my folks. Our families were friends. This wasn't one of those "arranged" matches by our families, the kind that were common in Europe. But I knew right from the start that Mary was "my girl" and that we would eventually marry. We have been married for almost forty years and we have known each other for almost fifty years.

The "other" woman in my life was Sister Mary M. Joella.

She planted the seed in me that would grow and grow until it eventually was harvested in my career. She was a teacher in Our Lady of Perpetual Help grammar school. I had to go to OLPH because my own parish, Our Lady of Peace, didn't have a school. But on Sunday, I had to go to church at Our Lady of Peace because it was predominantly an Italian parish.

Sister Joella didn't know very much about sports, but she knew enough to use it as a teaching vehicle. She was wise enough to recognize that sports was important to us, and she took the interest we had and exploited it. I remember her telling us stories about Knute Rockne of Notre Dame. I was fascinated by those stories and I am sure something registered within me and I must have decided, then and there, in my adolescence, that I wanted to emulate Rockne and become a coach.

I played all sports as a kid but not very well. Whatever was in season—baseball in the spring, football in the fall, basketball in the winter—enveloped me at the time. And there were the typical city street games like stickball, box ball and stoop ball. I played them all, pickup games and in makeshift organized leagues with teams.

I used to have to get up early on Saturday mornings, around six o'clock, and wash the floors of the store, clean up, sweep, put the stock on the shelves and get everything ready so that Pop could open for business by eight o'clock. As I said, Pop never understood my passion for sports. He thought it was a waste of time, that I never would amount to anything. But Mom was understanding and sympathetic. Often, she would let me take an early slide and she would finish my chores because I had a game under the 59th Street Bridge. Mom somehow realized how important it was to me and recognized how necessary these games were to my growth.

With the end of the Depression, Pop's business improved. We weren't wealthy by any means, but there always was food on the table and enough money for clothes, a new suit and a new pair of shoes for Christmas and Easter. And there usually was enough left over for entertainment.

Occasionally, when school was out, I would take the subway or bus across town to the Times Square area where the big bands would be playing at the Paramount Theater, the Strand, the Roxy, or the Capitol. Those were the big theaters in my day where, for twenty-five cents, you would see a first run movie and a stage show, usually featuring a big band like Glenn Miller, Harry James, Count Basie, and the Dorseys, Jimmy and Tommy. Benny Goodman was my favorite because he played the clarinet and I fancied myself a clarinet player.

In the summer, I would take the train up to Yankee Stadium for a baseball game. A group of us would go up. The subway was a nickel and a bleacher seat cost about 50 cents. I'd pack a veal cutlet sandwich on Italian bread for my lunch and I'd buy a Coke and we'd sit in the bleachers and watch Lou Gehrig and Joe DiMaggio and Bill Dickey and Lefty Gomez and all those great Yankees stars. We always managed to get there early enough to watch batting practice and infield practice. If there was a doubleheader, that would be a bonus, but we'd still hope for extra innings because we never could get enough of it.

Just about everybody in our neighborhood was into baseball. In those days, the city of New York was fortunate to have three major league teams, the Yankees in the Bronx, the Giants in Manhattan, and the Dodgers in Brooklyn. In our neighborhood, there were fans of all three teams and constant arguments and discussions about the relative strengths and weaknesses of the teams. The rivalries were unbelievable; those arguments would rage well into the night.

Even though the Giants were closest to our neighborhood and probably should have been our favorite team, most of the people where I grew up were Yankees fans, for one important reason. It was an Italian neighborhood and the Yankees had all the great Italian stars like Tony Lazzeri, Frankie Crosetti, Phil Rizzuto, and, of course, the great Joe DiMaggio. Even Pop took pride in the fact that the Yankees' greatest star was Italian. Pop didn't care about baseball, he didn't understand it, and he never went to a game, but he always asked about DiMaggio.

Although he never took to spectator sports, Pop had a great sense of family, an instinct for keeping the family together. Some fathers would take their sons to baseball games. Pop took me hunting and fishing. That was his way of spending time with me, sharing a common interest with me.

The last time we went hunting was with Willis Reed. Willis liked Pop and Pop liked Willis. Pop liked him because Willis shared three interests with him. He liked to hunt. He liked to eat pasta. And he liked to drink wine.

Just before Pop died in 1981, the three of us went hunting in upstate New York, where I have my basketball camp. Willis was working with me as an unpaid assistant basketball coach at St. John's. It was in March, two months before Pop got sick. He died that December. Now whenever I think of him, I think of that hunting trip and it always brings a smile to my face. Pop was 80 at the time, but he still loved to hunt.

We're walking along on our hunting trip looking for game and a flock of birds flew overhead. Willis lifts his gun, "Bam-bam," he knocks down a bird. Now it's my turn. "Bam-bam." I knock down a bird. Then pop raises his gun. The birds were so close, I could have hit them with a frying pan. Pop fires. "Bam-bam." He misses.

"Damn cartridges," he says. "They don't make them like they used to."

Now Willis gets an idea.

"Let's let Pop get a bird," he says.

Willis slips off and hides behind a tree. Pop raises his gun and fires again. "Bam-bam."

As he fires, Willis fires from behind the tree at the same time and knocks down a bird.

"Hey, Pop," Willis says. "Nice shot."

And Pop just looked at Willis and said, "Boola-sheet."

As busy as he was with the store, Pop always had time to take me hunting and fishing when I was a kid.

As a kid, I developed another passion that would stay with me forever: my love for good Italian wine. I acquired my taste for vino from my grandfather and namesake. He was quite a character, Grandpa Luigi, a large and gregarious man who worked as a stone mason. He did a lot of work in Sardinia and was involved in the construction of the railroad for the French government. He helped build a railroad in Africa, from Djibouti to Addis Ababa.

Grandpa Luigi was the patriarch of the Carnesecca family in every sense of the word; a typical, old world Italian grandfather. He had a great influence on me, although he never came to the United States and the only time I spent with him was that little more than a year we lived in Italy. I regret I didn't get to know him better.

Grandpa Luigi had a ritual that after dinner he insisted on the family remaining seated while he led us in saying the rosary. He was a very religious man, a daily communicant, and he had great faith in the rosary. I was forbidden to leave the table and go out and play until the rosary was said.

Grandpa loved his wine. He made it himself. Great wine. Even as a kid, I was allowed to have a little glass of wine with dinner. You have to understand that wine was part of the culture in Italian homes, the centerpiece of many of the meal time conversations. Winemakers—and that included my grandpa—took great pride in their wine. There always were debates on who made the best wine, who had the best barrels, the best vines, the best grapes. It was a badge of honor to have the reputation of having the best product.

I would say they were as avid about their wine as New Yorkers are about sports—and just as fanatical. Wine was the staple of every household. They used it in the preparation of soup, they used it for medicinal purposes, I even heard about them washing babies in it.

So, it was only natural that children would be weaned on the family-made wine. It is part of the culture that children were permitted to have a small glass of wine with dinner. Not enough to get light-headed, or slightly tipsy, but enough to acquire a taste and learn the difference between the various wines.

And this was a tradition that lasted a lifetime. My great grandma Jiuditta, for example. Every night, after dinner, she would tell my uncle Anthony to bring her a fiasco of wine and she would take it to her room and lock the door and drink her wine. Every night. And after about a half hour, you would hear singing coming from her room. Great grandma Jiuditta lived to the age of 96. I don't want to say that wine was responsible for her longevity, but the wine certainly made her declining years much happier.

Pop tried to make wine, too, but it never seemed to come out right. Then Pop would make excuses for his wine. He would blame the barrels, blame the grapes, blame the moon, the stars, the weather. He would blame everything but himself. Pop didn't make good wine. He made good vinegar.

When it was time for me to go to high school, Mom and Pop decided I should go to a Catholic school, St. Ann's Academy, even though it cost money to go there and the public schools were free. It turned out to be the right choice as far as my future was concerned. St. Ann's had an excellent, active athletic program. I tried out for both the baseball and basketball teams (the school didn't have a football team or I would have tried out for that, too). I was equally bad at both sports.

I was a little better baseball player than I was a basketball player, which isn't saying very much. I made the baseball team as a second baseman, but I was a lousy basketball player. The worst. It took me three years to make the junior varsity and when I finally made it, I think it was because the coach, Brother James, realized I loved the game so much that he put me on the team. I didn't play very much. Instead, I learned the game from the seat of my pants, which, looking back, may have been a blessing in disguise.

A lot of baseball managers and basketball and football coaches were not great athletes themselves. Many of them were bench warmers like me, and I think sitting on the bench, observing, helps you learn the game better. You learn it from a coach's point of view. You certainly have more time to study what's going on out there when you're not out there.

For some reason, despite being a better baseball player, I always liked basketball more and I studied basketball more than baseball. I knew even then that I wanted to be a coach, another Knute Rockne, and my own coaches must have known that, too. That may be why they put me on the jayvee. I was coaching even then in a Catholic Youth Organization league. Funny, I always got more enjoyment and more satisfaction out of coaching than I did out of playing. Probably because I was such a terrible player.

I had four coaches at St. Ann's who influenced me in my future career. Three of them were of the cloth: Brother Joe Leo, Brother Maurus James and Brother Terrence. The other was a man named Dave Tobey, a wonderful little guy and a great coach who also became an outstanding basketball referee and later was elected to the Basketball Hall of Fame.

My high school days were the best days of my life. I had a wonderful time at St. Ann's, but that had to come to an end and I had to start thinking about choosing a college that would help me fulfill Pop's ambition that I become a doctor. But it was a decision that would have to be postponed temporarily. Something else came along that took precedence. It was called World War II.

TWO

World War II and College

When World War II broke out, I was a sophomore in high school. I remember that December 7, 1941, so vividly, as if it were just a few years ago. It was a Sunday afternoon and I was listening to the New York Giants' football game when the broadcast was interrupted by a news bulletin.

I heard the announcer say that the Japanese had bombed Pearl Harbor and that the United States was at war with Japan. I was sixteen years old, what the hell did I know? I didn't even know where Pearl Harbor was. Besides, I was too young to go into the Army and, for all I knew, the war would be over by the time I graduated from high school two years later.

Pop was so proud to be an American citizen and so much in love with his adopted homeland, he would have been more than willing to serve in the Army if called. But he was forty, too old for service when the war broke out, and he was the head of a household and the sole support of a family, so he was rejected. Meanwhile, I went about my routine of going to school, helping out in the store, and playing ball.

When I graduated from St. Ann's in June of 1943, the

27

war was still on. In fact, it was in full flower, so I knew I was going to have to delay my college career indefinitely. I was going to be eligible for the draft in August. I wanted to serve my country, but I also wanted to try to avoid getting my little Italian head shot off. It was my buddy, Joe Fecci, who came up with the perfect solution.

"Join the Coast Guard," Fecci said.

He had joined the Coast Guard and he was pounding the beach at Atlantic City, a nice, soft job.

"They'll give you a dog and all you have to do is pound the beach," Joe said. "And you'll be home every weekend."

It sounded like a good deal to me, so a couple of friends and I went down and enlisted in the Coast Guard and Joe was right. For the first three months, I was assigned to Manhattan Beach, Brooklyn, for boot camp and I was home every weekend. A pretty good deal.

All of a sudden boot camp is over and they send me to New London, Connecticut.

"Hey, Joe, what happened?" I said to Fecci.

"You need a little more training," he said. "Don't worry."

Well, New London is not that far away and I'm still getting home every weekend, but after a few more weeks they send me to Boston. I'm getting farther and farther away from home and Fecci is still pounding the beach with the dog in Atlantic City.

"Don't worry," he said. "You'll be OK. I know you're going to be great. Trust me. You'll see."

A couple of days later, I get my orders to go to Alameda, California. I didn't come back until three years later and when I came back, Joe Fecci still was pounding the beach with the dog in Atlantic City, the sonofagun.

Instead of Atlantic City, I went to Perth, Australia; Calcutta, India; Ceylon; Luzon; Okinawa; Guam; New Guinea; Yokohama; and Tokyo. I hit them all.

"Those are the breaks," was all that Joe Fecci, my buddy, could say.

I was on a troop transport. We carried the 82nd Airborne from Calcutta to Okinawa. They were supposed to jump on Japan the day the war ended. That's the day we arrived in Okinawa. We had two escorts, Canadian frigates, zigzagging ahead of us. Torpedoes crossed us, but we never were hit. We were pretty quick—22, 23 knots an hour. Obviously, the word hadn't reached us or the enemy that the war was over, but that was the closest I got to seeing any action. As far as I was concerned, that was as close as I wanted to get.

A lot of guys got to play sports during the war, but I never did, except for an occasional pickup baseball or basketball game. But I did wind up in an outfit that had a few former professional boxers. Big name fighters, people like former light heavyweight champion of the world, Gus Lesnevich, and former lightweight champion, Lou Ambers, and a couple of good local club fighters from Brooklyn, Patsy Giovanelli and Danny Kapilow. And Johnny Colan, whose real name was Coliani and who had twice fought the former light heavyweight champion of the world, Anton Christoforidis.

I introduced Johnny to his wife on the trip from Los Angeles to Calcutta. She was a nurse named Jo. They were married after the war.

That reminds me of the time I introduced somebody else to his wife, but they were already married.

Mac Hodesblatt was a very successful high school basketball coach from Thomas Jefferson High School in Brooklyn. He was a wonderful man, very dignified and scholarly, in addition to being an excellent basketball coach. He had some good teams at Jefferson and turned out some outstanding players, many of whom we recruited for St.

John's. Probably the best of Mac's players, and the most successful, were Tony Jackson and LeRoy Ellis, both of whom were great players for us.

One night I went to Madison Square Garden with a doctor friend of mine. Mac Hodesblatt was there with his wife. I wanted to introduce my friend to Mac, so I went over to him. After exchanging pleasantries with Mac and his wife, I started making the introductions.

"Mac," I said, "this is Dr. Sullivan. Doc, this is Mac Hodesblatt. And this is Mrs. Hodesblatt. Mr. Hodesblatt, this is Mrs. Hodesblatt."

And that's how I introduced Mac Hodesblatt to his own wife.

It was quite a kick serving in the Coast Guard with all those great boxers and getting to know them. I never did any boxing myself, but I always loved boxing. Still do. I can remember as a kid going to the Queensboro Arena under the 59th Street Bridge. For a buck, you could see a full card of eight bouts with some good fighters in those days. I would go to the St. Nicholas Arena in Manhattan and MacArthur Stadium in Newark for the fights.

Occasionally, I went to the famous Stillman's Gym in Manhattan. It cost fifty cents to get in and you could sit there all day and watch fighters train. All the great ones trained at Stillman's. I used to get a big bang out of seeing them up close.

I remember seeing Rocky Graziano in Stillman's Gym once. He was wearing a green robe that had the words "The Rock" inside a boxing glove on the back. He came out wearing the robe to start his training for the day and everybody started hollering and applauding him because he was such a big favorite in New York in those days. I saw a lot of great fighters in Stillman's. Beau Jack, Freddy Apostoli, Tony Canzoneri.

Boxing and baseball were the two big sports of my

youth. Boxing had its neighborhood, ethnic rivalries, and baseball was big because we were fortunate to have three major league teams in New York City. Professional football still had not made it big and neither had professional basketball. College football and college basketball actually were bigger than the pros, but you almost had to have an affiliation with a college to really appreciate it and get into it.

I spent three years in the Coast Guard and it wasn't such a bad life. It was clean and relatively safe. We ate well and we lived fairly well, especially compared to the Army guys. My ship was a Navy ship, the *General H. B. Freeman, AP 146*, that was manned by the Coast Guard and that transported Army and Air Force troops and had a Marine guard, so all branches of the military were on that one ship. We used to feel sorry for the Army men. "Poor Dogies," we called them. They had it rough, but we lived almost in luxury by comparison. We had clean sheets and plenty to eat. In fact, there were a couple of guys from New Orleans in our outfit, Italian guys, and they were always making pasta and pizza. It was almost like home.

Here it is more than forty years since I was in the Coast Guard and I still get letters from guys who were in my outfit. They'll read about St. John's in the newspapers or they'll see me on television and they'll write to me.

When I was in New London, I was hurt playing in a pickup basketball game. Since I couldn't perform my normal duties, they put me to work in the hospital operating room. I really liked that. I did microscopic work on slides and tropical disease work. I liked it so much, it made me begin to think that maybe Pop was right, that I should be a doctor. But I could never have been a good surgeon. Bad hands.

The war ended and I got my discharge and was ready to start college. Pop still was determined that I should be a doctor. "Be somebody," he kept saying. I didn't want to disappoint him even though my heart really wasn't in it. To pacify him, I enrolled at Fordham University and took a premed course. I hated it. I really was miserable. I just knew this wasn't for me.

All my close friends—Dick McGuire, Patty Digilio, John Cannizzo, Danny Buckley—were at St. John's. Danny talked me into leaving Fordham.

"Lou," he said, "come to St. John's. It's home. All the guys are here."

That's when I decided to leave Fordham and transfer to St. John's. Pop wasn't too thrilled with the idea and I hated to break his heart and ruin his dream, but he never said anything. I think he knew how unhappy I was and that I'd never be a good doctor.

I started at St. John's and from the first day, I knew Danny Buckley was right. It was like home. Danny even convinced me to go out for the basketball team.

"But Danny," I argued, "I can't play."

"That's all right," he said. "They'll put you on the team, anyway. You'll sit and watch."

I did get to play on the baseball team, your typical good-hit, no-field second baseman. I always could hit. Not a power hitter, more of a spray hitter, singles and doubles. But I was a lousy fielder. I never turned a double play in my life. I was all right on pop flies, but I couldn't pick up a ground ball to save myself. If you're a second baseman and you have to have a weakness, it's not a good idea for that weakness to be ground balls. If the ball was hit in the air, I had a shot. But hit one on the ground and I had no chance. I used to wear a helmet in the field. I got hit on the head once. I couldn't put on my hat for a week.

Frank McGuire was my baseball coach because, as I have mentioned, in those days, the basketball coach had to double and coach baseball, too. One day, we had a practice scheduled at Dexter Park. We get to the field and McGuire starts giving out instructions.

"Mike, you pitch batting practice. Johnny, you hit fly balls to the outfielders. Jimmy, you hit ground balls to the infielders. Jack, you go to the bullpen and warm up the pitchers. And Lou, you . . . er, Lou . . . er . . ."

"That's all right, coach," I said. "Just give me a broom and I'll sweep out the locker room."

Another time, we were playing against City College and I had three hits in my first three times at bat. Now, it comes time for me to bat for a fourth time and McGuire calls me over. I figured he wanted to give me some instructions. Instead, he tells me he's putting in a pinch hitter for me.

"But coach," I argued, "I've got three hits in this game."

"I know," he said. "That's why I'm putting in a pinch hitter, you little runt. I figure the law of averages is against you."

I was really ticked off. Not only did he take me out for a pinch hitter, he was putting in Jack Gimmler, who was the worst hitter I ever saw. And what does Gimmler do? He hits a pop fly that starts out about 50 feet foul. Suddenly, a gust of wind grabs the ball and carries it back into fair territory. The ball drops in short left field, two runs score and Gimmler, the big stiff, winds up on second base with a double.

The next day, in the newspaper, there was a headline: "Gimmler's Double Wins for St. John's."

I couldn't believe it. Some double. The big bum carries that clipping around in his wallet to this day. Every once in awhile, he takes it out and tells people about his big, clutch double, just to burn me up.

We actually had a hell of a baseball team in 1949. We made it to the College World Series, the first time a St. John's team had ever gone to the World Series. The star player on our team was Jack Kaiser, now the director of athletics at St. John's. Kaiser was named College Baseball Player of the Year that year.

More and more, I began to realize that basketball was my game. Not as a player, mind you. I still couldn't play and I hadn't grown any in the Coast Guard. In college, I was the same height as I was in high school, which is the same height I am now—five feet, seven inches.

But I loved the game and I studied it carefully from my seat on the bench. Dusty DeStefano was coaching the jayvee team and Joe Lapchick coached the varsity in my first year in school. The following year, Lapchick left to coach the New York Knickerbockers and Frank McGuire took over as head coach of basketball and baseball.

Frank is such a great judge of talent, he recognized immediately that I couldn't play. Of course, that didn't take any great perception. But he also recognized my love for the game and my enthusiasm. He began to put me to work, refereeing the scrimmages, scouting players, and scouting our opponents.

"Just tell me everything you see," McGuire would say. I'd sit up in the crow's nest, high atop the old Madison Square Garden, and scout the teams that were coming up on our schedule. I loved it. It made me feel important and it made me feel like I was making a contribution. The more I did it, the more I loved it. I liked it even better than playing.

It was Frank who gave me my chance, who kept me involved. I've never forgotten that. Thanks to him, I always saw the game from a coach's point of view. Frank allowed me to express myself. I would go with Dusty DeStefano and him to look at players they were recruiting. I was always allowed to express my opinion, and I was allowed in our dressing room to listen to the coaches talk. I walked into practice anytime I wanted to. I refereed the practices. It was like having an internship. I was getting an education through the eyes of a coach. And I was convinced that this was my calling.

I even got a chance to coach the freshman baseball team. Frank McGuire was coaching the varsity, but he took sick and Dusty DeStefano took over the varsity and made me the freshman coach. That's when I decided baseball wasn't for me. Most of the games were played in the spring, April and May, which can be blustery and cold and rainy in the Northeast. I hated those days, it was so cold. But you could see the field from the coach's office and many games, I just sat in the office, raised the venetian blinds and coached the team from there. If I waved my handkerchief, that was the bunt. If I took my hat off, that was the steal. Simple.

One day, I was coaching at third base (it must have been at least 80 degrees) and guys started stealing every time they got on base. I couldn't figure out what was going on. Every time a guy got on, he would take off for second.

One guy got thrown out and I started chewing him out.

"What are you running for?" I exploded.

"You gave me the sign," he said.

"No, I didn't," I said.

"Yes, you did," he insisted.

I happened to have a rash in the area of my crotch that I kept scratching. The steal sign happened to be scratching my crotch. So the more I itched, the more I scratched, and the more I scratched, the more the runners attempted to steal.

Another time, I had to go to Dexter Park for a tryout early in the season. I hated being there, but I had been told to go and to start trimming the squad because it was too large. I show up and it's freezing and I'm just thinking to myself that I want to get this over with as fast as I can. So, I walk over to a group of players and I take one look and I couldn't believe my eyes. They were the worst looking group of so-called athletes you can imagine. Half of them were wearing glasses and some had sneakers, no spikes. Some of them had makeshift uniforms from their neighborhood teams, with their socks falling down, and some had no uniforms at all.

I am a firm believer that to be a good ballplayer, you have to look like a good ballplayer, so I look around at this motley group and I begin making my cuts.

"You," I said, "you're cut. You, you and you. Out. You and you, take a hike."

All of a sudden, I look up and here comes a familiar figure. It's Bob Tierney, who was athletic director and coach at Queens College.

"What are you doing, Lou?" Tierney said.

"I'm just cutting my squad, Bob," I replied.

"Your squad is down there," he said, pointing to a group of players at the opposite end of the field. "This is my squad that you just cut."

One of my players on that freshman team was a young centerfielder from South Jamaica named Mario Cuomo. He was a hell of a player, a great competitor, and a good street fighter. He was a pretty good hitter. Not much power, but a good line-drive hitter and a good hitter for average, kind of like me. We also had something else in common. Like my pop, Mario's father also operated a grocery store.

Besides his talent, Mario also had a stubborn streak. When McGuire wanted to convert him from centerfield to catcher, Mario would hear none of it. He quit the team rather than catch. Later, he played a season of minor league ball in the Pittsburgh Pirates' organization before deciding to give up his dream of playing major league baseball and returning to St. John's Law School. To this day, McGuire still gets ribbed for being the only coach to force a future governor to quit his team.

I graduated from St. John's knowing what direction I

wanted to take in my career. But I needed a job and none were available. More than that, I needed to earn some money. That's where a couple of friends, Eddie Murphy and Jimmy Sullivan, did me a big favor. At least I thought they were doing me a big favor. Murphy and Sullivan were well-known basketball referees in the New York area and they were asked to provide officials for the Puerto Rico summer league. They knew I was available and that I needed a job, so they asked me if I wanted to go to Puerto Rico to work as a referee.

I told them I didn't have very much experience as a referee except for scrimmages at St. John's and some pickup games.

"That's perfect," Murphy said. The next thing I knew, I was on my way to Puerto Rico. At 1 P.M. I'm on a plane and at 5 P.M. that same day, I'm in Sixto Escobar Stadium officiating a game with 7,000 people in the stadium and the place going wild.

Three minutes into the first quarter, I make a call. How was I to know I had just called a foul on the local hero? Before I could turn around, I'm being showered with missiles from the stands. They threw bottles, rocks, mangos. Being a college graduate, I worked the second half wearing a helmet.

Somehow I managed to escape that rather inauspicious debut with my life. The next day, I had to travel across the island for a game in Ponce. We drive up to the arena and I noticed the place is surrounded by barbed wire.

"What's this?" I asked, a little anxiously.

"Don't worry about it," I was told. "The fans here are very enthusiastic. It's only a precaution."

I got through the first half with no problem. Two minutes into the second half, I called a technical foul on the high scorer of the home team. That did it. Before I knew it, I had a riot on my hands and I'm standing in the middle of a dozen cops protecting me from people trying to get at me. The cops hustle me out of the arena and back to my hotel and the only thing I could think of was, "You did me some favor, Jimmy Sullivan and Eddie Murphy."

The next day, I called for a meeting with the commissioner of the league, a guy named Garcia.

"Mr. Commissioner," I said. "You may have noticed that I'm having a few problems. I'm wondering if there is anything you can do to help me out. What would you do in my place?"

Without blinking an eye, Commissioner Garcia said, "If I were you, I would quit and go back home to the United States."

I can take a hint as well as the next guy. I took the next plane out of there. I'm nobody's fool.

THREE

Coaching at St. Ann's

Timing is everything in life. I came back from Puerto Rico with no job and with no prospects of getting one. Just a few months later, I got my big break. Paddy Gleason, who was coaching at my high school alma mater, St. Ann's Academy, got sick and I got a call from my old high school coach, Brother Hugh Arthur.

"How would you like to coach our basketball team?" he asked.

Was he kidding? This was a dream come true, coaching my old high school team. It took me about two seconds to make up my mind and tell him yes, I'd love it.

My coaching career didn't exactly get off to a rousing start. For one thing, the first day I walked into the dressing room, the players looked at me as if to say, "Who is this guy? Is this our leader?" They all towered over me and I wasn't much older than they were. I admit I didn't strike a very imposing figure for the players I was supposed to lead.

I'll never forget the first game I ever coached. It happened to be in Madison Square Garden. It was the custom in those days for local Catholic high schools to play in the Garden as the preliminary to the Knicks, who were coached by Joe Lapchick. We played St. Nicholas of Tolentine from the Bronx, which was coached by the late Rocco Valvano, the father of North Carolina State coach, Jimmy Valvano.

I had inherited an excellent, veteran team led by one great player, Danny Powers, and he hit seven jumpers in a row at one point and made me a winning coach in my first game. This was easy. This was going to be fun. Nothing to it. We then went on to lose our next eight games and my kids must have been thinking, "Some coach. What the hell does he know?"

Fortunately, thanks to players like Danny Powers and Larry Tierney, we turned things around and finished with a winning record. I'm afraid if we hadn't, my coaching career might have ended almost before it got started, and Lou Carnesecca never would have been heard from again.

Paddy Gleason decided not to return to coaching, so the job was mine for a second year and we won the New York City Catholic High Schools championship, something St. Ann's had never done before.

By now I was hooked on basketball. I also was a married man, Mary and I having gotten married after my first season of coaching. Supporting a wife on a high school coach's salary wasn't easy. Fortunately, Mary had been working since she graduated from high school.

Mary had a good job with ASCAP, American Society of Composers, Authors and Publishers, the songwriters' union.

Once I had the job at St. Ann's, it was total immersion in basketball. I forgot about almost everything else. It became a passion with me, a fixation, a mania. I don't think I spent one day, or part of a day, when I wasn't thinking about basketball. If there ever was a fanatic, I was it. And it wasn't for the money. I could have made more money cutting salami in Pop's store. Basketball was just something I loved and couldn't get enough of.

Mary was great. She understood my love for the game.

Here we were newlyweds and I think I took her to every doubleheader at Madison Square Garden. My basketball education even extended to the summer. I attended every clinic I could get to. I took down every note, attended every lecture. It was basketball, basketball, basketball. Even after our daughter, Enes, was born, I would leave Mary and the baby and go off for a couple of weeks during the summer to continue my education, to serve my internship. I paid my dues. I spent time in the laboratory. I did work on the cadaver, so that when I opened it, I knew what I would find inside. I had already been there.

For two summers I worked as a counselor at Clair Bee's All-America Camp in Cornwall-on-Hudson in upstate New York. It was the granddaddy of basketball camps and every few days Adolph Rupp would come through, or Red Auerbach would come through, or Red Holzman, Frank McGuire, Ken Norton, Dudey Moore, Ben Carnevale. And, of course, the master himself, Clair Bee, who may have had the finest basketball mind of all. Bee was the first coach I ever saw use changing defenses. On offense, he preached the concept of letting the ball do the work and of taking good care of the ball; he stressed movement, trying not to go to only one guy, to use all five players on the court. These concepts are all very much in use today, but Bee was teaching them forty years ago. He was truly a basketball genius, far ahead of his time.

I got to meet all the great coaches of the day, to listen to them, talk basketball with them, ask them questions. For me, it really was a fiesta of basketball.

The man who had the greatest influence on me in those days was Buck Freeman. At St. John's, Buck had coached the team known as "The Wonder Five" in the twenties and thirties. It was the Boston Celtics of its day. Ironically, the Wonder Five was made up of four Jewish kids and one Polish kid representing a Catholic university.

Buck taught me so much, not only about basketball, but about people and about life. He was working up at Clair Bee's camp and, consequently, I had access to him any time I wanted. I listened to him and I learned so much from him.

Buck was a big, striking man. He stood six feet, four inches tall. He had a shock of pure white hair and he had this big, booming voice and he spoke the language to perfection. He was a scholar in Latin and Greek who could have been a great educator. But basketball was Buck's life. He never married. Basketball was his wife and his family. It's just about all he lived for and he never tired of talking about the game, expounding on his theories. That was fine with me. In me, Buck not only had a captive audience, but an eager and willing listener. I asked him thousands of questions and I soaked up everything he said.

Buck had trouble sleeping. He could often be seen at 11 P.M., midnight, 1 A.M., just walking the grounds of the camp. As a counselor, one of my duties was to pull a watch at night to make sure the kids didn't destroy the camp. On those nights, I'd take the opportunity to sit with Buck and talk basketball.

During one of these sessions, Buck first told me his theory about coaches being worth no more than 15 to 20 percent of a team's success. He stressed the fact that it's the players who make a team a winner. I have never forgotten that. It was a humbling thought, but I have tried to remember that throughout my career. A coach is only as good as his players. A bad coach can win more games with good personnel than a good coach can win with inferior personnel.

Like Clair Bee, Buck Freeman was truly a basketball genius, a coach who was years ahead of his time. He had been Frank McGuire's coach at St. John's and he became

Frank's guru, his teacher and his right hand. Buck was like a father to Frank. Even Frank will admit that he owes much of his success to Buck Freeman and, as a result, wherever Frank went, Buck always had a job. You have to respect Frank for his loyalty.

The story is told that soon after McGuire took over at North Carolina, they were playing a game and getting blown out. And Frank was sitting on the bench calmly, his arms folded. But Buck was going out of his mind.

"Frank, they're killing us," Buck said.

"I know, Buck," Frank replied softly.

"They're hurting us off the boards," Buck continued.

"I know, Buck," Frank said.

"Frank, what are we going to do?"

"We're going to get better players," Frank said.

And they did. They recruited players from New York, guys like Lennie Rosenbluth, Joe Quigg, Pete Brennan, Tommy Kearns and they were the nucleus of the team that beat Kansas with Wilt Chamberlain to win the national championship in 1957.

Not only was Buck Freeman a great coach, a genius, he was one of the most beloved figures around in his day. People just seemed to take to him. They used to say he should have been a priest. The man was brilliant. When he gave a lecture on shooting, I thought I was listening to a pathologist break down the human anatomy. With his classical background, he used words derived from the Latin. He talked about the rotation of the ball, the arc of the shot—"That's arc, not arch," he would say—and he talked about the "flex of the muscle extension." He could really hold your attention when he talked.

He also had a sense of humor, a kind of dry wit, and the ability to take the wind out of your sails with one sentence.

One day I had put on brand new shorts, and I thought I looked pretty good in my shorts and polo shirt. I went up to Buck and said, "Hey, Coach, how do I look?"

He just looked down at me from his great height and said, "Louis, the only guys who should wear shorts are guys who are tall, blonde, and good looking. You fit none of these categories."

To this day, I won't even wear shortie pajamas.

Needless to say, my internship at Clair Bee's camp and my talks with Buck Freeman and all the other great coaches fortified me for my job at St. Ann's. And I needed all the fortification I could get in the Catholic High Schools Athletic Association, the league in which we played.

Let me tell you what it was like in this bucket of blood league. They not only wanted the ball game, they wanted your blood and your guts. I was just a kid and I had to coach against some tough veteran coaches like Chick Keegan at St. Francis Prep, Dick King at All Hallows and Herb Hess at St. John's Prep. It was like playing against Hitler, Mussolini, and Hirohito. That was some league. There was such great intensity and rivalry, but it was great preparation and a great experience for a young coach. If you could coach in that league, against those coaches, you could coach anywhere.

The courts were so small, the fans were practically on top of you. It was a tough league and it was especially tough to win on the road. When we played at home, if a visiting player had to go into the stands to retrieve a loose ball, our fans would hold him and keep him from getting back on the court.

One gym was so small, there was hardly any room under one basket. So they kept the door open and if you drove in for a layup, your momentum would carry you right out the door and into a yard, and you'd end up playing with four men.

Another reason it was so tough to win on the road was that the home team got to pick its own referees. If that ref didn't favor the home team, he wouldn't get picked to work again, so naturally he would bend over a little and favor the home team. How would you like to be playing on a visiting court and when a guy on the other team scores a layup, the referee tells him, "Nice shot"? It actually happened in that league.

St. Ann's hadn't beaten All Hallows at their place for years and one season we finally beat them. The fans were livid with rage. As I was walking off the court after the game, an old lady started hitting me over the head with an umbrella.

A couple of years later, we met LaSalle Academy, coached by my old buddy, Danny Buckley, for the Catholic High Schools championship of New York City. The game was at the old 69th Regiment Armory, where the Knicks used to play a lot of their home games in the early days, when Madison Square Garden was occupied by college basketball or the circus or the rodeo.

We came into the game with a record of 31-1 and we had already beaten LaSalle twice during the regular season, so we were heavy favorites to beat them again in the championship game. But I learned a great lesson that day: Never take anything for granted in the game of basketball.

We came down to the final seconds leading by one point and with the ball in our possession. All we had to do was run out the clock and the championship would be ours. LaSalle had this big, lumbering, 6-11 kid named Glynn. All of a sudden, he steals the ball, dribbles the length of the court and throws up a desperation shot at the buzzer. The ball rolls all around the rim and finally drops in and we get beat. I think it was the only basket this kid scored in his life and it cost us the city championship.

To this day, I remember the depression I felt after los-

ing that game in such a heart-breaking fashion. I thought
the whole world had come to an end. My wife's cousin,
Johnny Chiesa, was at the game and he waited for me and
took me home. As we were walking down the street, Johnny
put his hand on my shoulder tenderly and said, "Lou, don't
take it so hard. It's only a game."

I've never forgotten that. It has stayed with me for
almost forty years. I still live by that expression.

Another thing I'll never forget about that day is what
happened when I got home. It was the middle of a snow
storm, one of the worst storms in years. I figured I might
as well shovel the snow from the front of my garage. I'm
still upset after losing the game and this would be a good
way to cool down and get the game out of my system.

I start shoveling the snow and the next door neighbor
is standing there looking at me. He's not saying anything,
just watching me shovel the snow and smoking one of those
little Italian cigars. And I'm shoveling and shoveling. It's
snowing so hard, the more I shovel, the more I had to
shovel. I shoveled for two and a half hours trying to get my
car out of there.

Now Mary comes down and says, "What are you doing?"

"I'm shoveling the snow, what the hell do you think
I'm doing," I growled.

"Idiot," she said. "You shoveled the wrong garage."

I had shoveled the garage of the guy with the cigar. No
wonder the guy didn't say a word. I was so mad, I wanted
to punch the guy with the cigar and Mary, too.

FOUR

Assistant to Joe Lapchick

Soon after the end of the 1956–1957 season, I got a call one day from Jack Kaiser at St. John's. There was nothing unusual about that. Jack and I talked often. We had been friends for years, all the way back to when we were classmates at St. John's.

Jack had been an all-America baseball player at St. John's, an outfielder who probably could have had a career in professional baseball. Instead, he opted for a career in coaching. Pro baseball lost a good man, but the world of intercollegiate sports benefited from Jack's decision. So did the hundreds of young people who came in contact with this great, caring person and who were influenced by him.

In his early days on the coaching staff at St. John's, Kaiser wore many hats—freshman basketball coach, chief recruiter, freshman baseball coach, later varsity baseball coach. Eventually, Jack would give up coaching to become assistant athletic director to Walter McLaughlin, the school's long time AD. When McLaughlin retired, Jack was the logical, and perfect, choice to succeed him. Jack's my boss now. More important, I count him among my dearest friends.

When Jack called me, he still was involved in coaching. As I explained, we would talk often because not only were

47

we college classmates and friends, I was doing a little scouting for St. John's in those days. It was legal back then for a high school coach to moonlight as a college scout. Since St. John's was my alma mater and because of my relationship with Jack Kaiser, I was only too happy to do it. Besides, it meant I got to see even more basketball.

When Jack called, he asked me if I could stop by the school at my earliest convenience. I honestly had no idea what he wanted. I figured it was something to do with discussing prospects or setting up some scouting assignments for the following season. I lived not far from St. John's, so it was no inconvenience for me to stop there.

Jack took me for a walk, which I thought was rather unusual. But I still had no inkling of what was to come.

"How would you like to come here to coach?" Kaiser asked.

I was flabbergasted.

"We'd like you to be Joe's assistant," Kaiser continued and the more he talked, the more excited I got.

I really was stunned. Shocked, you might say. I just never imagined that this would happen to me. Certainly not so soon, when I was so young and inexperienced. I had just turned thirty-three and I had been coaching for only seven years. Surely, there were a lot of guys out there more qualified, more successful, more experienced. Besides, I barely knew Coach Lapchick. I had been around him a little when I was a student and I had been in his company as a high school coach, but I could hardly say I really knew him or had a relationship with him. More important, I didn't think he really knew me.

One of my first questions of Kaiser was to find out if this was something that met with Lapchick's approval. Jack assured me that it was. Naturally, I was flattered by the offer. Also naturally, I accepted. As difficult as it was to leave Molloy (St. Ann's had moved from Manhattan to Queens the year before and changed its name to Archbishop Molloy), I knew this was my big break. Every high school coach dreams of a chance to coach in college at one time or another in his career, especially when he's young, ambitious, eager, and cocky.

That described me to a T. In fact, I probably was too cocky for my own good in those days. Here I was a successful young high school coach who had just won the National Catholic High Schools championship for the third time. I thought I knew all the answers. Worse than that, I must have acted at times like I knew more than the guy I was working for, and he had spent fifty years in the game.

Joe Lapchick had been a great player in his day. He was basketball's first "big" man at six feet, five inches tall. He was the center of the legendary original Celtics, a semi-pro team and the best basketball team of its time. There were no organized leagues back then—this was years before the National Basketball Association. Instead, the Celtics toured the East and played against local pickup teams during the so-called dance hall days, when the basketball game was actually a preliminary to a dance. When the game was over, they would clear the basketball court, the band would set up, and the gym would be converted to a dance hall. That was basketball in its infancy. The dance was a greater attraction than the basketball game, but it was a chance for these players, these early pros, to bring their new game before the public.

Joe never played college basketball for the simple reason that he never went to college. Very few did in his day, which was sometime between World War I and the Depression. He never had a college degree, but he had wisdom and intelligence you cannot learn in a classroom. I'm convinced that Joe Lapchick, given the opportunity of education, could have been anything he wanted to be—college professor, corporation president, elected official, statesman, ambassador—that's how wise and intelligent he was. He chose to be a basketball player, and later, a basketball coach. He even turned down an opportunity to play professional baseball—I hear he was an outstanding pitcher in his day—because he loved basketball so much. Basketball would be our common ground, despite the differences in our upbringing, our ages, and our ability as players.

When his Celtics days were over, Joe turned to coaching. He was hired by St. John's to replace Buck Freeman as coach. By his own admission, Joe knew very little about coaching.

"I was thirty-six years old," he once told a sportswriter, "and I knew I didn't have much playing time left and I had no idea what I wanted to do. Then I got a call from Father Rebholz of St. John's, who said he wanted to interview me for the job of basketball coach."

This was 1936 and he was paid $2,500 to coach freshman, jayvee, and varsity basketball and varsity baseball.

"I had a strange feeling," Joe later said. "Here I was a grammar school kid, trying to teach college kids. I had put them on a pedestal. But the day finally came when I had to put up or shut up. I was in awe of these mental giants standing there in front of me, waiting for me to give them some words of wisdom.

" 'All right, boys,' I said. 'Go out and shoot.'

"They shot and shot and then it was five o'clock.

" 'OK,' I said. 'That's all for today.'

"For two weeks, all they did was shoot, shoot, shoot. I didn't know what else to have them do. I didn't know anything about drills. We never used that stuff with the Celtics. The only practicing we did was shooting. I had read somewhere that a coach should be high in the crow's nest while his team was practicing so he could look down on them. So I climbed up to the top seats in the old DeGray Gym and I just walked around, looking at them.

" 'You phony so-and-so.' I said to myself. 'You don't have the slightest idea what to do next. What are you doing here, anyway? You don't belong here.'

"Finally, after two weeks, Jack Shanley, the captain of the team who became Chief Police Inspector, came to me.

" 'We're tired of shooting, Coach,' he said. 'Can we do something else?'

" 'All right,' I said. 'Let's scrimmage.'

"After the first few weeks, Father Rebholz asked one of the players what he thought of his new coach.

" 'Father,' he said. 'He stinks. He doesn't know anything.'

"And he was right."

Joe Lapchick may have started out not knowing anything about coaching, but he sure got the hang of it in a hurry. In his later years, he was a brilliant strategist, a great tactician, and an outstanding clinician. But Joe's forte always was his ability to handle people, to motivate them, and to get the most out of them. He was a master psychologist.

After coaching at St. John's a few years, Lapchick left to become coach of the New York Knickerbockers in the early days of what would become the NBA. That's when I was still a student. Later, he came back to coach at St. John's, which was a few years before I came aboard as his assistant.

When I came along, I was all full of myself and knowing all the answers. I must have annoyed Joe, but to his credit he never took my enthusiasm away and he never was afraid to allow me to express myself. He would just listen to me. And the more he listened, the more I expounded my theories.

One day, I suppose when he could take it no longer, he said to me, "All right, I listened to you, now you listen to me. Get this through that thick head of yours. Sometimes you go off in all different directions. That's OK. Your enthusiasm is wonderful, but you have to learn how to control it. You have to learn how to channel it properly."

We had an excellent team once that I felt was being torn apart because two of our best players could not get along. I suppose there was a rivalry between them that was growing into jealousy. They had both been the big man on their high school team, and the big men in the city of New York in their senior year, one in the public schools league, the other in the Catholic schools league. They both came to us with the idea of being the big man on our team.

I felt there was no room for this sort of jealousy on a team. In fact, I thought it was counterproductive and that it could destroy the chemistry on the team. I thought that would hurt us eventually and I told Joe so. I suggested that we get rid of one of the two players for the good of the team.

"Anybody can do that," Lapchick said. "That would be the easy thing to do, but it would also be the coward's way out. It might destroy the kid we get rid of and it might not even make us a better team. No, our job is to get them to play together and blend."

He was right, of course. If you have diverse personalities on a team—and you almost always are going to have that with any group of people, especially kids—you can't get rid of them all. The coach's job is to get those diverse personalities to blend. And Joe was a master at that. Those two guys never got to like one another, their jealousy still existed, but Lapchick took that rivalry and used it to benefit the team. And that team won both the Holiday Festival and the National Invitation Tournament that year.

I learned a lot from Lapchick by the way he handled that situation. I learned a lot from him in so many areas but especially how to deal with people—with the media, with officials, with school administrators and, especially, with players.

Joe hated geniuses, guys who thought they were so good, so smart. He was a humble man himself and he hated guys who thought they were better than everybody else. He used to love to beat those guys. He had a subtle way of bringing guys down to earth, taking the wind out of their sails. He did it to me often.

I remember one time in particular, after Lapchick had retired and I was coaching the team. It was after the 1966–1967 season and I had been named Coach of the Year by the Metropolitan Basketball Writers Association. They had an awards dinner at a Manhattan hotel. After the dinner, some of us went to Danny's Hideaway for a few drinks. There were Jack Kaiser, Jack Gimmler, Marty Satalino, who had been an outstanding basketball and baseball player at St. John's when it was possible to play both sports, and Joe and I.

I got a double dose of humility that night. When we walked in the place and handed the hatcheck girl our coats and hats, Gimmler said to the hatcheck girl, "Do you know who that is? That's Carnesecca."

"Carnesecca," she said. "Carnesecca. I know that name. Oh, yeah. Doesn't he run the grocery store on 62nd Street?"

Later in the night, as we were about to leave, Joe reached into his wallet and took out a little card and handed it to me.

"Here," he said. "Take this and put it in your wallet. Carry it with you all the time and when you think you're pretty smart, read it."

The card said: "Peacock Today; Feather Duster Tomorrow."

I guess you can say that was Joe Lapchick's philosophy in life, that you can never get too self-satisfied with what you have accomplished. I carry that card with me to this day.

Joe was always so low key, I don't think he realized

how good a coach he was. He was damn good. In his final season as coach, we played for the championship of the National Invitation Tournament in Madison Square Garden. I never saw a team so fired up as that one. He never spoke to the team, never asked them to win this one for him because it was his final game as coach. He didn't have to.

We were heavy underdogs to Villanova, but we won the game and the championship. Rather, Joe won it with his presence and by what he meant to the kids.

I remember reading about the game the next day and something team captain Ken McIntyre said stayed with me.

"Coach never asked us to win this game for him," Kenny said. "He could have. He could have psyched us out of our minds. He could have told us he really wanted to win this one and asked us to win it for him, but he never did. All season he told us to win for ourselves. He could have asked us to run through a brick wall and we would have said, 'Which wall?' "

A lot of Joe's old players were there that night to see his final game. People like Carl Braun, Harry Gallatin, Fuzzy Levane and Dick McGuire. Each of them played for Joe and every one of them became a coach.

I remember Harry Gallatin coming into the dressing room after the game and telling Joe, "That's some retirement. If I could ever get my guys to play their guts out like that for me, I'd be happy. They gave everything, from their toes to their hair."

After the game, Joe kept repeating over and over, "What a way to go out . . . what a way to go out. . . ." We went to Mamma Leone's after the game to celebrate and we stayed up most of the night and Joe kept saying it over again, "What a way to go out . . . what a way to go out. . . ."

I remember thinking if I ever had a team that played

as hard for me as that team played for Joe, I would know I had reached the ultimate in coaching.

I can't tell you how many nights I sat up with him, playing every game he ever coached over and over. It would be four in the morning and I'd be nodding off and he'd be wide awake. He'd see my eyes close and he'd hit me a rap.

"Hey," he'd shout. "Wake up. There was the time in Buffalo. . . ."

One day in August 1970, I gave a clinic in the Monticello, New York, area. I finished the clinic and I said to myself I'm this close, I'll go and pay the old coach a visit. He was at Kutsher's Country Club, where he spent most of his summers. His friend, Milt Kutsher, would invite Coach there to be a goodwill ambassador for basketball.

I get there about 10 P.M. and I meet him at the bar. We start talking and drinking, talking and drinking. Now, I'm all over the country again. It's two o'clock, three o'clock, and I'm replaying every game he ever played and every game he ever coached. It gets to be four o'clock and we finally say goodnight. And I still have to drive back to my camp. I get into my car and I didn't realize I had drunk as much as I did. I don't know how I got back to the camp. Instead of driving on Route 17, I caught myself driving across a field.

That was on a Thursday. Sunday morning, I get a call from Richie Lapchick, Joe's son.

"Lou," Richie said. "Dad passed away."

I had known he had a heart condition, but it still came as a shock. I had been with him only three nights before. At least I got to see him and spend some time with him before he died. I'm glad I decided to pay him a visit. I don't think I would have forgiven myself if I had been so close and not seen him and then he had died without my seeing him.

I still miss him; I think about him often. I think about some of the expressions he used, some of his philosophy. I still carry in my wallet the card he gave me that night in Danny's Hideaway. His picture hangs in the most prominent place in my office. He was such a great man. I admired him so much.

FIVE

Head Coach,
St. John's

I spent seven wonderful years as Joe Lapchick's assistant. I learned from him, I enjoyed being with him, and I came to regard him as one of the truly great people I have ever known, both as a coach, a mentor, and a person.

I have to admit the two of us made an Odd Couple of basketball—Joe, a lofty six feet five, me a diminutive five feet seven. He was "The Big Indian" and I was "Little Looie" and we were a funny sight walking together. "Mutt and Jeff," the writers called us after the comic strip of the same name. I looked up to him in more ways than one.

The rumors started during the 1964–1965 season. At the time, St. John's had a little-known and generally unpublicized policy that retirement was mandatory for any employee who reached the age of sixty-five. This rule was in force for everyone—professors, maintenance men, priests, administrators, secretaries, and basketball coaches.

Lapchick's sixty-fifth birthday was coming up and stories began to pop up in the newspapers that the university was going to invoke the mandatory retirement rule on Joe and that I was going to take over as head coach. I knew none of this, only the rumors I read about in the newspapers and I didn't pay any attention to them. Nobody connected with the university had ever so much as mentioned that Joe was being retired, let alone that I was in line to be his successor.

One story especially angered me because it was so preposterous. This story contended that the main reason St. John's was going to invoke the mandatory retirement age on Lapchick was that it was afraid I was going to start getting impatient and begin to look around for a head coaching job at another school.

Nothing was farther from the truth. I wasn't eager for Joe to retire. While it was true that I was getting feelers from other schools and I had several opportunities to go someplace else, I wasn't going anywhere. I was happy at St. John's. I enjoyed working with Joe and I would have stayed no matter how long Lapchick stayed. Where was I going? I knew the New York area. All my friends were here, my family was here. To pick up stakes and go somewhere else wasn't something I wanted to do or that I believed to be in my best interest and the best interest of my family. If the time ever came when Joe did retire, I would have wanted to be considered to replace him. But there was no guarantee from the school and no ultimatum from me.

As it turned out, Joe had no choice. A rule is a rule and the university invoked the mandatory retirement. It was announced that I would step up and be his successor. As much as I wanted Joe to continue, it was out of my control. I thank God that I never left St. John's and things worked out as they did.

Lapchick didn't want to retire and that made things a little difficult at first. But the university had the rule and it was made very clear that there would be no exceptions. Even a famous, popular, and successful coach like Joe Lapchick was to be treated no different from a professor of logic or the janitor.

I have reason to believe Joe was a little bitter with some

people at the university, but it never changed our relationship. I had his blessing as his successor and he even told
me so.

After he retired, Joe said to me, "Lou, I won't come to
the games and the reason I won't come has nothing to do
with you. I don't want people to think I'm looking over your
shoulder. I don't want the press to see me and begin asking
me questions and interviewing me. I don't want to take the
spotlight away from you. You deserve it and I want you to
have it."

I appreciated what he was doing. He didn't come to
the games, except for rare occasions, and some people might
have interpreted that as evidence of bad blood between us.
Not so. We spoke frequently. He was very supportive and
very helpful. If I had a problem, a question, he would be
the first person I'd go to. And it didn't just have to be something about basketball. I could go to him with anything and
I often did, and he'd always have some very wise advice.

The seven years I spent with Joe were an education in
many ways. I was fortunate that I didn't go someplace else
or get the job earlier. I wasn't ready. But when I did get the
job, I was prepared for it. There was nothing new. Because
of Joe's willingness to give me a free hand on so many
things, to encourage me, and because he was so secure,
anything that came up I had done before.

The time had finally come for me to reach back and
draw from the knowledge I had acquired through the years
from all those great basketball minds I met at clinics and
camps, and to implement it all into a formulated plan of
my own. I soon realized that my basketball education had
not stopped once I became head coach at St. John's. In
many ways, it was only beginning.

I had all that knowledge poured into my brain from
Joe Lapchick, Buck Freeman, Frank McGuire, Dudey Moore,
Ben Carnevale and all those other great coaches, and I sup-

plemented that knowledge with more clinics and camps and more conversations with the younger breed of coaches.

Nobody was more influential on my coaching career, or more helpful, than Bernie (Red) Sarachek, from whom I would formulate my offensive strategy. Red would become my mentor, my coaching guru, and my close friend. He's a dear man with a heart as big as a battleship. I consider him almost like a father to me. Not only are we good friends, for more than thirty years, Red and I have been partners in a basketball camp. The true test of our friendship is that, despite the camp, we're still friends.

The name Red Sarachek may not mean much to people with no more than a layman's interest in basketball. He does not have the recognition and high visibility of some of the other coaches I have talked about. But mention his name to other coaches and they know exactly who he is, what he has done, and how brilliant a basketball mind he has.

The reason Red does not have the recognition from the general public that he deserves is that he never coached at a major university, a so-called basketball power. But any coach will tell you, Red has a brilliant offensive mind and his credentials as a coach on every level are staggering.

I first met Sarachek in 1953, when I was coaching at St. Ann's. Dolly King introduced me to him. Dolly had been a great player at LIU in the thirties, the best big man in the area at the time. Later, he played pro ball for Red in Scranton before becoming an outstanding college referee.

"Lou," Dolly said, "this guy can help you."

That's how I first met Red. I started listening to him talk and I was very impressed. He had a way of breaking things down to the barest essentials. He said things with such simplicity, they were easy to grasp. We have been friends ever since, and I have been listening to him and learning from him ever since.

Red coached for years at Yeshiva University and he got more out of players with limited ability than any coach I know. Before that, he was Red Holzman's coach at Franklin K. Lane High School in Brooklyn. He won championships in the AAU. He coached in the old ABA, which was the precursor to the BAA and NBA, and he won championships in 1949–1950 and 1950–1951 with the Scranton Miners, where he produced outstanding players such as Pop Gates, a great, great player of his day; Nat Militzok, who played for the Knicks in the first game they ever played, against Toronto; Eddie Younger, who played for LIU; Bob Kelly; and Dolly King. Red also coached in the New York State League, which is the oldest professional league.

So you can see, he has spent his life in the game of basketball and he has a tremendous background as a coach. As a player, Red played at NYU. He said he was a good player, but Red says some things that you have to take with a grain of salt. His knowledge of basketball, however, is not one of them.

On a personal level, I think the reason Red and I are so close and have remained friends for so long is that besides our mutual love for basketball, we are a lot alike. He's disorganized, absentminded and a lousy businessman, just like me.

For years, Red operated a sporting goods store in Brooklyn near where Ebbets Field used to be. If I tell you there was no worse businessman in the world than Red Sarachek, I'm not exaggerating. Red was too involved in basketball, his head swimming with all his theories to have a head for business.

He used to sell equipment and uniforms to many of the high schools and colleges in New York. He never kept books and often he didn't know who had paid him and who hadn't. Many times, he forgot to collect his bills.

One time, a coach told him he wanted to have t-shirts

made up for his team. This coach wanted to give nicknames to his squad, as motivation for a big game coming up. The coach came up with the nickname "Alley Cats," for his defense and he asked Red to make up t-shirts with the name "Alley Cats" on them. Red says fine and a few days later, he delivers the shirts. The coach opens the package and what does it say on the shirts? "Pussy Cats."

Another time, Cesare Rubini, the Italian basketball coach, happened to be in the United States. He mentioned that he wanted new uniforms for his team, so I put him together with Red. Rubini describes exactly the kind of uniforms he wants, the color, the design. Beautiful uniforms. Red takes the order and promises to ship the uniforms to Italy. When the uniforms arrive, Rubini couldn't believe his eyes. The shirts were perfect, exactly how he wanted them. But the pants were something else. Instead of basketball pants, Red made up football pants and sent them to Italy.

That's Red Sarachek. He's really unconscious, except when it comes to the game of basketball. It's amazing how he can zero in and focus on basketball yet, in business, he is a different person. If you ever went into his store, you wouldn't believe it. It was chaos. You never could find anything. He had t-shirts that came in the customary sizes of small, medium, and large. But Red couldn't be bothered sorting them out and keeping them separate, so he took a stamp and marked them all "regular" and sold them all the same.

Friends would come in and he'd say, "Take this. Here, give this to your kid." He was always giving things away. If he collected everything owed to him, he would be a multi-millionaire today. But Red never had a head for business and he never really cared about money. He loves people and he enjoys chaos. In that way, he reminds me so much of my father. He has many of the same qualities as Pop. Maybe that's why we became such good friends.

You want to talk about chaos, you should spend some time at our camp. It's called the Carnesecca-Sarachek camp, but it should be called Camp Chaos. Who's coming, who's going; who has paid, who hasn't paid. We had no idea what was going on. A kid would be there one day, the next day he'd be gone. We didn't know why, he just left. We'd see some new kid and Red would say to me, or I'd say to him, "Where did he come from?"

We had no records, no books. For twenty-one years, we had the same staff. And we never made any money until 1987, when we finally hired an administrator.

The camp is in upstate New York, in the town of Sidney. We've been there a few years and I think we're settled there now. We've had the camp all over, but we had to keep moving every few years because the people didn't want us back.

The best camp story is one that Jack Gimmler likes to tell. So I'll let him tell it:

"It's the first day of camp and it's total chaos. I'm sitting in the outer office, acting as the registrar. Lou and Red are inside in the inner office. A couple comes in, Mr. and Mrs. Sullivan, with their son, Danny, and they're going to register him for camp.

" 'Wonderful,' I'm thinking. 'My first customer.' So I give them the forms to fill out and tell them, 'That will be $125.'

" 'Oh, no,' the mother says. 'Coach Carnesecca said there would be no charge.'

"I go into the back office where Lou and Red are and I tell Lou there's a Mr. and Mrs. Sullivan outside with their son, Danny, and they say they were told there would be no charge. Lou confirms it and I go back to finish the registration. The walls are paper thin and you can hear everything being said in the inner office. I'm talking to the Sullivans and I can hear Red yelling at Lou.

" 'Damn free loaders,' he's saying. 'No good cheapskates. What the hell are you doing? How can you let this kid come for free? How are we supposed to make any money on this camp if you're going to let all your friends come here for nothing?'

"A few minutes later, Red comes out. 'Oh, Mr. and Mrs. Sullivan, welcome. How are you? Nice to have you with us. Of course, there's no charge for you.'

"Now, about ten to fifteen minutes pass and here comes another couple with a kid.

" 'We're Mr. and Mrs. Brown and this is our son, David. Mr. Sarachek invited David to his camp as his guest. He said there would be no charge.' "

As a basketball coach, especially with the offense, Red Sarachek has no peer. He taught me a lot about being creative with the ball, how to get players to do things individually, how to make guys look better. The idea Red tried to put across is to prepare a player for any eventuality and to allow him to retain his individuality within the framework of the team.

You might give a guy a play, Red said, but you never knew what defense the opposition was going to employ. So you have to give your players the freedom to express themselves and to have variations on that play. A player has to be allowed to create according to the defense, to react to the defense. You can't play basketball unless you know what the defense is going to do. Is your man playing you too tight? Is he dropping off? Is he playing too far to the left? To the right? Is he playing defense at all? The player, Red preached, has to have the option of changing the play depending on the defense. I learned things from Red thirty years ago that I still use today. That's how far ahead of his time he was.

If Red Sarachek was my offensive guru, much of my defensive thinking I got from Ben Carnevale, a Hall of Famer. Ben did such a great job coaching at the Naval Academy, but like Sarachek, he never got the recognition he deserved because he didn't have the talent at Navy that other coaches had in other schools. This was years before Navy could recruit a player of the stature and size of a David Robinson. But like Red Sarachek, Ben Carnevale made the most of the limited talent he had.

Every year, I would make it a point to take my team down to Annapolis to scrimmage against Ben's team just before the start of our season. I knew Ben's team would play tough defense and they would give my guys a hard time. It would be the toughest defense they saw all year and that would sharpen them up for the season.

This, too, is something I inherited from Joe Lapchick, who also had great respect for Carnevale's defensive genius. I remember taking our team to Annapolis in November of 1963, just before the start of our season. We made the trip by bus and we got all the way down there, got off the bus, and learned that President Kennedy had just been shot in Dallas. Naturally, the scrimmage was canceled. We just got back on our bus, turned around, and went home. It was a long, sad journey back to St. John's. Those were three days in which the world stood still.

SIX

My First Five Years at St. John's

The time between my appointment as Joe Lapchick's successor and my first game as basketball coach at St. John's University went quickly. There was so much to do and so little time to do it—picking my assistant coaches, meeting with my players, setting up scouting assignments, getting my recruiting in order, setting up a practice schedule, cutting the squad. Fortunately, I had done most of this under Lapchick, so it wasn't that I was going in cold, but the time just flew by and the next thing I knew, it was time for my first game.

No matter how much preparation you have had, how many years you have been involved with the game as a high school coach and as an assistant, your first game as a head coach is always special and memorable. After all, there is only one first game in every coach's career.

Mine happened to be on the road, against Georgetown, in McDonough Hall. My first whack at the big time. The place was jumping. I mean it was going wild. And I don't mind telling you, I was scared to death.

So many things go through your mind before your first game. You want to be sure that you have thought of everything, that you have left nothing undone or unsaid. But when you come down to it, all you can do is work hard and prepare and try to cover all bases. In the final analysis, it comes down to the execution by your players.

My head was swimming with a lot of thoughts, mostly things I wanted to cover before sending my team out on the floor. You can't appear too nervous because your team picks up on that and it could reflect how they play. You certainly don't want to seem unprepared to your players because that could cause them to lose their respect for you.

It's like when the game comes down to crunch time, you're leading or trailing by just a couple of points and you call a timeout to set up a play. You better have an idea what you want to do and what you want to say when your team huddles around you. You don't want to appear indecisive, scared, pessimistic, or beaten to your players. The same applies to your final words in the huddle before the start of the game. It's very important that you, as a coach, give off an air of confidence, a sense of being in control.

With that in mind, I gathered my players around just seconds before the start of my very first game as a head coach for St. John's. It has been my custom, since I began coaching and right up to the present, to gather my players around me in a pregame huddle, have everybody touch hands, and lead them in a short prayer to Our Lady of Victory.

What I say is, "Our Lady of Victory, pray for us. Amen." Nice and short. I have been saying that for more than thirty-five years. I can say it in my sleep, I have said it so often.

It's not that I was shook up or anything, you understand, this being my first game and all. But I gathered my players around me, we put our hands together and I started to lead them in prayer to Our Lady of Victory.

"Oh, my God, I am heartily sorry for having offended thee. . . ."

Instead of my usual prayer to Our Lady of Victory, I had inadvertently started saying the Act of Contrition, which is what Catholics say for absolution of their sins after the priest has heard their confession.

Some of my kids just looked at me like I was going out of my mind. Others started to laugh. I finally caught my mistake and, trying to suppress a smile and remain cool at the same time, I quickly went into my usual prayer to Our Lady of Victory.

That was an embarrassing and inauspicious debut if ever there was one. I wouldn't be able to live it down for years. Fortunately, Bobby McIntyre hit a jump shot in overtime to break a tie and we went on to win the game. My college coaching career was off to a good start.

The early years of my coaching career at St. John's become a jumbled montage of games and players all blending together. In those days, the NCAA tournament was not what it is today. Not as many teams were chosen to go and it didn't have the national television exposure and the big buildup it has today. The National Invitation Tournament (NIT) was still competing with the NCAA for teams for postseason play. The NIT was played in Madison Square Garden and, as a local team that used the Garden as our second home, we had to try to keep both tournaments happy. As a result, in my first five years, we went to the NIT twice and the NCAA three times.

I can remember a seemingly endless parade of great games and great players in those early years.

We played a big game against St. Joseph's, which was rated number three in the country at the time. They were coached by Jack Ramsay and led by Matt Guokas. It was a big game not only because of St. Joe's rating, but because of what was going on in school at the time. It was a period of great unrest, student strikes, protests, demonstrations. At the time, we had an athletic moderator named Father

Casey. He was a redhead, a former athlete and chaplain in the service—a tough cookie if ever there was one.

I witnessed Father Casey perform one of the most courageous acts I have ever seen. A girl who was demonstrating came up to him and spit in his face, a symbol of her defiance of authority. It was almost like Our Lord being reviled by the Roman soldiers.

Knowing Father Casey, he would have wanted to haul off and hit the girl with the Mary Ann, his right hand. I could see him tense up, the back of his neck get a flaming red. Father's courage was in showing restraint. Imagine some kid spitting in your face. It took all his courage and restraint not to belt her. He just walked away. It was the best thing he could have done. What would have been the easy thing to do? Hit her with the Mary Ann. But that would have been a disaster. We might have had a riot on our hands. His restraint not only was courageous, but it was the right thing to do.

We wound up beating St. Joseph's and, in some strange way, I believe that helped diffuse the tense situation of the protests. Sports can do that. People get caught up in team spirit and good feeling after a big win and it helps dissipate your anger.

There were other big games in those first five years. I remember, in the 1968–1969 season, playing the number one, two, and three teams in the country all in the same week. First, we played North Carolina, the third-rated team, in the semifinals of the ECAC Holiday Festival at Madison Square Garden and beat them, 72–70. That put us into the championship game a couple of days later against UCLA, the number one team in the country, which had Kareem Abdul-Jabbar (Lew Alcindor at the time), Sidney Wicks, Curtis Rowe, Mike Warren, and Lucius Allen. One of the great college teams of all time. They beat us by 18.

A few days later, we played Davidson, rated number

two in the country, at their place. We beat them when Billy Paultz hit a jump shot at the buzzer. In less than a week, we had played the top three teams in the country and beaten two of them.

I remember a game in which we beat Brigham Young on a shot at the buzzer by Albie Swartz. I remember Albie Swartz. The B'nai B'rith named him to its all-Jewish college basketball team. Trouble was, Albie wasn't Jewish. But he did live on Jerusalem Street, near a synagogue. Maybe that's why the B'nai B'rith picked him.

In 1969, we traveled all the way to Hawaii to play in the Rainbow Classic. In the first round, we beat Iowa, the Big Ten champion, on a jump shot at the buzzer by Jimmy Smith. Now we have to play LSU and the great Pistol Pete Maravich, who was literally a scoring machine. At the time, he was averaging about 45 points a game.

Now I have to prepare a way to stop the Pistol. I come up with an idea. I tell Jimmy Smith, "You're going to play the Pistol, but here's what I want you to do. When he gets the ball, I want you to just turn your back and walk away from him."

Smitty looked at me like I was crazy.

"Yeah," I said. "You heard me. Just walk away from him."

There was a method to my madness. Everybody had played him every way. Tight. A box-and-one. Triangle-and-two. They tried every defense in the world, and he was still getting his 44, 45 points a game. I figured what did I have to lose? I had heard that sometimes you can take away a guy's concentration when you do something unorthodox, something he's not expecting.

So, that's what we did. The game starts, the ball goes to Maravich and Smitty turns his back and walks away. Pistol looks at him as if to say, "What? Are you nuts?"

He throws up a shot. He misses. I look at Smitty and

I give him a knowing wink. We did this the entire first half and all Pistol got was about eight points, well below his average. We walk into the dressing room at halftime and I say to Smitty, "We got him, right? OK."

In the second half, they throw Maravich the ball, Smitty walks away as he did in the first half, and, bang, Pistol hits a jumper, a real three-point shot. Again. And again. He hits five long jumpers in a row. Now I start yelling to Smitty, "Get up on him."

Then I put two guys on him. Three. Four. He broke the tournament record and they beat us by 10. In the post-game talk, I told the kids, "Who the hell's idea was it using that defense?"

There was another big game at Syracuse, when we had Lloyd (Sonny) Dove. A large contingent of St. John's fans made the trip to Syracuse and when the game began, they let loose a flock of doves.

And I remember the funny moments. We were playing at West Point one night against Bobby Knight's Army team. As usual when we played Knight's Army teams, the game was like World War I, hand-to-hand combat. First they take the lead, then we take the lead, then they go ahead, then we go ahead. The lead kept seesawing back and forth like that all night and the more intense it got, the more I'm running up and down along the sidelines, yelling instructions at my players, imploring them, twisting, turning, stretching, kneeling. I was really caught up in the game.

So was Bobby. His language was worse than ever. The Superintendent of West Point was at the game, entertaining a military VIP and his wife. The Superintendent was getting more and more embarrassed by the minute at Bobby's language. He's glaring at Bobby, but Bobby is still yelling and screaming and cursing.

Finally, the Superintendent yells down, "Coach Knight, please watch your language."

Bobby looked up at the Superintendent, made a gesture to him that said "We're Number One" and continued yelling, screaming, and cursing. I think that's when Bobby was gone from West Point. It's a good thing he got the Indiana job, or he might never have been heard from. I know he was not going back to Army.

Anyway, this game is vicious and hard fought. Bobby is yelling and screaming and cursing. I'm running up and down the sidelines, begging, pleading, kneeling, stretching. I think Bobby and I crossed on the sidelines, so that at one time, I was in front of his bench and he was in front of mine.

I have this habit of running up and down, moving down from the bench, coming back and sitting in my seat. That's exactly what I did this time, but when I sat down it was on something soft.

Now the referee, Hal Grossman, comes over and says, "Hey, Lou, what the hell do you think you're doing?"

"What do you mean what am I doing?" I said. "I'm coaching the frigging basketball game."

And with that, I turn around and look down and I see I'm sitting on some woman's lap. I was just about to ask her what the hell she was doing in my seat when Grossman led me away. The woman is looking at me like I'm some kind of nut and I was so embarrassed. I mumbled a quick apology to the woman and went over sheepishly and took my seat on our bench. What else could I do?

SEVEN

Coaching the Nets, 1970–1973

My first five years as head coach at St. John's seemed to just fly by. I enjoyed them tremendously. This is what I always wanted to do and, to make it more pleasant and rewarding, we had more than our share of success—a five year record of 104–35, a postseason tournament all five seasons.

I didn't feel that I had conquered the world or that I had accomplished all that I could at St. John's. Not by any means did I think that. But when the Nets made me an offer to leave college and join the pros, I jumped at the chance. I did it for two reasons.

Money? Yes. And no. I'd coach for nothing, but I'm not fooling anybody. The money was good. Fifty thousand dollars a year for five years, guaranteed. In those days that was a great deal of money. I was forty years old and I had made very little money as a high school and college coach. The money wasn't the primary thing, but I felt I owed it to myself and to my family when the Nets made such a flattering and lucrative offer.

If you ask me the difference between coaching in college and coaching in the pros, I could give you all kinds of differences—the travel, the number of games, the ability of the players. If you ask Mary the difference between coaching in college and coaching in the pros, she'd say with inflation, it's $200,000.

The other reason I took the Nets job is something most people might not understand. Pride and ego. I think anybody who coaches in high school and college always has that secret desire to find out how good a coach he could be in the pros, coaching against the best players in the world. I was no different. I was curious to see how I would do as a professional coach. It was a great personal challenge. If you spend your life in sports and are any sort of competitor, sometimes the challenge becomes the overriding factor in decisions such as these.

Actually, I had been invited to join the Nets a year earlier than I did. But my contract with St. John's extended through the 1969–1970 season. I could have gone anyway. They would have let me out of the contract. But I just couldn't do it. I felt I had to honor my contract and my commitment to the kids at St. John's. I told the Nets if they could wait a year, I'd come over. They agreed to wait. What was more surprising to me was that the press never got wind that I was all set to leave St. John's and coach the Nets.

Another reason I was eager to go is that my role was to be as both coach and general manager, which meant that I was going to be responsible for all personnel decisions. I wouldn't have to rely on the judgment of others. I could pick my own players, make whatever trades I felt were necessary and generally control my own fate. That made the job even more tempting. A coach likes to be in that position.

At the time, the Nets still were playing in the American Basketball Association (the merger with the NBA was a few years away) and they still were playing on Long Island, just a few miles from my home. (Eventually, they would move to New Jersey, but that wasn't in the offing back then, or it might have altered my decision.)

I stayed with the Nets for three seasons and I would say we did fairly well. We made the playoffs all three years. More important, I learned some valuable lessons that would help me when I returned to college coaching.

Lesson number one came in my first season: One player can make a significant difference in a team. We had acquired Rick Barry, one of the greatest offensive players ever to play the game. Single-handedly, he changed us from an also-ran to a solid contender for the ABA championship. That season, in the playoffs, we played what remains with me as one of the most exciting, most intense series of games I have been involved in. And it produced one of the greatest victories of my coaching career.

We had finished in third place during the regular season and met the Kentucky Colonels in the playoffs. Kentucky finished with the best record in the league, 68–16, but we beat them and knocked them right out of the league championship. Barry was sensational in that series. He averaged almost 50 points a game and came as close to being a one-man team as you can be in a team sport.

Our next opponent was the Virginia Squires, led by Dr. J, who was the best all-around player in the league. He had torn up the ABA that year and he, and the Squires, kicked the hell out of us in the first two games. It looked like we didn't have a chance against them. That's when fate, and modern technology, intervened to give us a needed reprieve.

The third game was to be played in the brand new Nassau Veterans Memorial Coliseum in Uniondale, Long Island, but the building wasn't ready and we had to wait nine or ten days for the workmen to complete it before we could continue with the series. The Squires were hot and they had momentum going for them. They obviously would have preferred to play right away, but we couldn't. And the long layoff helped cool them down while it helped us rest and regroup. It reminded me of the old slogan of the Boston Braves in the forties, "Spahn and Sain and two days of rain."

Rain was not the factor in our behalf, but the construction delay served the same purpose and we beat the Squires four of the next five games to knock them out of the championship and put us in the ABA finals.

The final game was so intense, the victory so emotional, the players and our fans just went wild and I believe that series helped establish the Nets. I can remember Pam Barry, Rick's wife, being so excited with our victory that she wound up in the shower with us after the game, clothes and all. I have no idea how she got there, but players were being tossed into the shower with their uniforms on and the next thing I knew, somebody had thrown Pam into the shower, too. It was wild.

We got to the ABA finals against the Indiana Pacers, led by George McGinnis. It was another great series and we went to Indiana for game six, trailing, three games to two. If we could beat the Pacers on their court, we would get to play the seventh game at home, where we were especially tough to beat.

We're leading by two with seven seconds to play. But Freddy Lewis of the Pacers steals the ball, goes in for a layup, makes it and gets fouled. Now we're down by one point. The rule in professional ball at that time was that the team getting fouled in the last two minutes gets to take the ball out at midcourt. So we take a time out to set up the final play.

Everybody in the building knows who's going to get the ball. Rick Barry. The Pacers know Barry's going to get the ball. The players on my team know Barry's going to get the ball. My mother, who doesn't know a basketball from a bocci ball, knows Rick Barry is going to get the ball.

So we set up the simplest of plays. We send Rick Barry around the block. There's nobody near him. Not only is he going to get two, but if you come up on him, he's going to get three. Troop Washington takes the ball out of bounds and he throws a beautiful pass, right on the money. Rick takes his eye off the ball, it hits his thumb, and on the third bounce it goes out of bounds. Goodbye championship.

After the game, we have a press conference.

"Well, gentlemen," I say. "It's only a game. We had a great season. The sun will come up tomorrow."

And everybody was saying look at what a great sport that Carnesecca is. He knows how to handle it.

I walk into the dressing room to talk to the players.

"Fellas, don't worry about it," I say. "It's only a game. We had a great season. I'm proud of every one of you. Go home and have a great summer. I'll see you next year."

"What a guy," they're saying. "Didn't yell at us. Wasn't mad. Great guy, that Lou."

Now I'm walking out of the arena. The fans are all around. I wave to them, shake their hands, smile.

"Yay, Lou," they're shouting. "What a sport. What a pro. Knows how to lose. Have a great summer, Lou."

That night, at 11 o'clock, in my room on the eleventh floor of our hotel, our trainer Fritz Massman had to stop me from jumping out the window.

The next season Rick Barry had left us and without that one player, we lost fifty games. We managed to make the playoffs anyway, but without Rick we had no chance and were eliminated right away. That's the lesson I learned. The players are everything. Nothing else changed, but take that one great player away and we were just an ordinary team. It drove home the lesson that I, as a coach, was nothing without that player.

I had learned another valuable lesson early in my Nets career when I refused to sign Julius Erving. Julius had decided to leave the University of Massachusetts and turn pro before his class had graduated. He very much wanted to play for the Nets because he was from Long Island and he would be playing in front of his family and friends. There was nothing illegal about what he wanted to do, but I was opposed to it on ethical grounds, perhaps because my background was in the college game. I believed then, and still do, that most kids should stay in school and get their degrees before becoming professional.

Julius came to my office and practically begged me to sign him. I told him I couldn't take him. I wouldn't feel right about depriving UMass of his services. I stuck to my guns even though I realized he was such a great player and that he was ready to play professional ball. I knew he would be a big star in the pros and he certainly would have been a big help to us. Dr. J was adamant. So was I. The next day he signed with the Virginia Squires.

I had three shots at Dr. J and didn't get him. I had recruited him when he came out of Roosevelt High School on Long Island, a relative unknown. It's hard to believe now when you realize what he became, but when he got out of high school, only three schools were interested enough to recruit him—Hofstra, UMass and St. John's. None of the other schools knew much about him but we did because he was practically in our backyard. He might have come to St. John's, but UMass invited his high school coach along with him and that's what made him decide to go there.

Soon after he signed with the Virginia Squires we had another shot at him. The Squires must have been having financial problems because before he had even played a game for them, we could have had him for cash. Maybe they didn't know what a great player they had in Julius. I did, but we still didn't sign him.

Can you imagine? I had three shots at the great Dr. J and blew them all. That's how smart I was. If I had taken him with the Nets who knows, I might still be coaching in the NBA today.

Now that it's too late, I realize that I made a big mistake not signing Erving for the Nets. Not because he turned out to be one of the greatest players the game of basketball has known. I was wrong on ethical grounds. I was stopping this young man from making a living and that was wrong. I had no right to impose my values and my ethics on him. It was entirely his choice. What he was doing was completely legal, and he might have had very good reasons for wanting the money that I didn't know about. Who was I to say he shouldn't take the money? Who was I to insist that he go back to school and get his degree? That was his decision, not mine.

I just never realized it at the time. I thought I was acting in the young man's best interests, but I had no right to do that. I have since changed my thinking on that subject. Years later I had a similar situation with another great young player, only this time, I was on the other side of the fence.

After the 1986–1987 season, Walter Berry had one year of eligibility left at St. John's. But he was under a great deal of pressure to file for hardship and make himself eligible for the NBA draft. It was not an easy decision for Walter to make, choosing between the money he could make in the pros and the chance to be the premier player in the country. Walter needed the money badly to help out his family and he wrestled with his decision for days before the deadline for filing.

He came into my office one day and told me about his dilemma. He was looking for guidance from me, but I was the wrong one to help him. I wanted him to return to school for the good of the team. If Walter had a dilemma, so did I. Did I want him back for the good of my personal record? Were all my motives based on selfishness? I still felt as I did with Dr. J, that a young man should finish school and get his degree. But could I be objective in the case of my own player?

Ever since the Dr. J case, I have this same conversation with all my kids who are eligible for the draft while they still have college eligibility remaining.

"If you're ready to turn pro," I tell them, "and your parents and you think it's the right thing to do because you need the money, then go. Don't worry about us. Don't worry about the team. We'll survive. Do what's best for you."

That's what I told Walter, although deep in my heart I felt he was making a mistake. I had talked with several general managers in the NBA and a couple of agents and each of them felt Berry would be wise to stay in school. He had won the John Wooden Award as college basketball's Player of the Year as a junior and the GMs I talked with felt his value would only increase after his senior year. They projected him to be the dominant player in the country again as a senior with a chance to lead us to the Final Four and get all the national exposure, attention, and recognition that went along with that. But how could I tell Walter all this without looking like I was thinking only of myself? So I said nothing. I let him make his own decision.

The day before he was to file for hardship, Walter said he stayed up all night wrestling with his decision. At the last minute, he got cold feet and didn't file. But by the next morning, he had changed his mind and he filed for hardship. That morning, Walter came into my office and told me what his decision was.

"Coach," he said, "I didn't think I could ever duplicate what I did last season."

He had a point. He wanted to play pro ball so badly, ever since he was a kid, and he was worried that he might not have as good a year as a senior as he did as a junior. Also, there is always the danger of injury that would decrease his value. For his family's sake, he said he had to turn pro. That was the bottom line and I couldn't, in good conscience, argue with him. I thanked him for coming to me first and I wished him well and told him I respected his decision.

As it turned out, he made a bad decision. Later, he even admitted it to me and said, "Coach, I never should have gone."

What happened is that he had a difficult time adjusting. He had hoped to be picked by the Knicks, where he would be home and playing in familiar surroundings and with his friends and family there to watch him. Instead, he was drafted by Portland, 3,000 miles from home, and things just didn't work out. He got off on the wrong foot with the people in Portland, then he was traded to San Antonio. That proved to be a better situation for him. He had a hard time adjusting at first, but he's adjusted now. He's going to be an outstanding pro.

He also got bad advice from an agent who told him he would get $400,000 a year for three years, a $1.2 million package. He got much less than that.

People say Berry's leaving cost us a chance at a national championship. Maybe it did, but I can't look at that. Forget that. More important, he may have cost himself $1 million by leaving school early. He could have scored 50 points a game, he was that good. He was a scoring machine. He could have been the number one or number two player in the country again.

In retrospect, at least he got it under his belt. It was an educational experience. He learned a lot. So he lost some money, so what? He'll make it up.

It was his decision. We didn't try to influence him one bit. He said, "Coach, I've got to go." And I said, "Walter, I understand. I wish you all the best." We were with him all the way.

He's such a good kid. He comes around when he's in

town. He's happy now. Things have worked out. He's twenty-two credits short of his degree but he'll get it. This was a kid I thought never would do it. We almost didn't even get him in school. But boy did he do it. He was so diligent, so conscientious. He never missed class. He proved us all wrong. I'm so proud of him.

To recap my three years with the Nets, I can see now that I wasn't prepared for the job. I don't mean technically. I was prepared technically, but mentally I wasn't ready for the professional life. I should have had two or three years as an assistant coach to learn the pro life and the mentality of the pro player. People tell me it would have been demeaning, a backward step in my career to be an assistant in the pros after five years as a head coach at a major basketball power like St. John's. I say so what. My ego isn't that big to consider it demeaning to be an assistant. It would have better prepared me for the pro game.

At the time, I couldn't fully understand that for my players, basketball is just a job. I was looking at it as a coach. I was too paternalistic, too used to dealing with high school and college kids. I might have been too close to my players. I was more concerned about a player's feelings than understanding that it's just a business to him. Tomorrow he might get fired and be out of work. Out of insecurity and self-preservation, loyalties are short. My problem was that I didn't understand all that. Maybe my players were more ahead of the game than I was. I was still operating like I was back in college.

Here I am busting my butt, giving a guy $500,000 a year, and he gives me half a day's work. That bothered me. Let's not forget these players were all-stars in college, all very successful before they came to me. This was their living and I was treating them like college kids.

A few years as an assistant would have helped me learn the workings and the thinking of the pro player—how to handle the diverse personalities, how to deal with the egos. It also would have taught me something of the lifestyle and the rigors of travel in the pros. Don't forget, we started in the middle of September and played until the middle of May. One year, we played 118 games as opposed to about thirty or thirty-five games in college. How would you like to have to make 118 halftime speeches?

It's too much to expect players to get themselves up for every game when they're playing 118 games. I didn't handle that as well as I could have.

Another mistake I made was thinking it was right to do both jobs, coach and general manager. I wanted to be in control. I didn't want anybody over me, and that was wrong. It's too much for one man. And it creates a problem with your players. Here I am as a coach, telling a player how good he is, trying to pump him up to perform better, then he comes in to me as a general manager looking for a raise and I have to knock him down. It's self-defeating. The guy I was trying to fight as a GM, I needed to play for me as a coach.

I would give any college coach going into the pros two pieces of advice. (1) Don't try to be both coach and general manager. It's too tough. (2) Don't go in cold. Get your feet wet first. Don't make the mistake I made. I simply didn't have the background in pro ball at the time.

On the other side of the coin, I don't regret my experience with the Nets. It was something I felt I had to do at the time and I'm glad I did it. Not just for the money, which of course, was a big help in setting me and my family up for life. I gained a lot from my pro experience, things that I have used since I returned to St. John's. I think it made me a better coach here at St. John's because it gave me a chance to reinforce some of the ideas I learned in the pro game when I returned to college.

For one thing, I learned about the player's ego. I also

learned from my experience with Rick Barry that it's the players who win, not the coach; that a coach is only as good as his players. And I came to the conclusion that you have to allow the players to express themselves on the court, to allow them to let their true personalities surface on and off the court. In college, a coach may have one guy who is so good, the coach will give him his own ball. In the pros, that same guy is going to have to split that ball with four other guys.

But the greatest lesson I learned is something I found out about myself. I am basically a teacher, much better suited for the college game than the pro game. I have had opportunities to go back to the pros, but I have declined. I feel I belong in college coaching and that's where I'm going to stay. I probably needed those three seasons in the pros to help me realize that I'm happiest right where I am, coaching at St. John's.

EIGHT

Back to St. John's

I never considered my three years in professional basketball a total loss. Far from it. It was a great educational experience that produced some good results, not the least of which were the financial rewards. While I can't discount that, it was never the primary factor in accepting the Nets' flattering offer. And it was not the most important byproduct of my pro experience.

I think I profited in other ways: a better understanding of the athlete's mentality, his hopes, his fears, his ambitions, his frustrations; I learned to give the player more latitude on the court—to free-lance, improvise, and do what he does best. The greatest lesson I learned, however, was about Lou Carnesecca; that I belong in the college game, that it is in college coaching that I am best suited and happiest.

I always will be grateful for the opportunity the Nets provided me, for the financial stability they helped me give my family and for the chance to learn a little more about myself. And I feel fortunate that St. John's asked me to return.

When I left St. John's, there was never any guarantee I would be able to return; no side deals that I could have my old job back simply for the asking. For all I knew, once I left the Nets, I might have had to take a job slicing salami. No doubt Pop would have liked that. My choice was to get back into coaching and when St. John's invited me back, I gratefully and hastily accepted.

There still were two years remaining on my contract with the Nets. If you want to get technical about it, they could have forced me to live up to my contract and I could have forced them to honor those remaining two years. The fact is, my parting with the Nets was a mutual agreement. I wasn't happy coaching in the pros. They knew I wasn't happy. So when we sat down to discuss our future relationship, it was mutually agreed upon that they would let me out of my contract and I would not insist on compensation for those two remaining years. It cost me money to leave, but my happiness and peace of mind were more important. The Nets saved money. I left an unhappy situation. So everybody was happy.

As it turned out, my old coaching job at St. John's was opening up. It seems that Frank Mulzoff, who had succeeded me and had done such a good job, was entertaining an offer from another school. He wanted to leave the New York area and he asked to be let out of his contract at St. John's. The university agreed, which left the job open. St. John's was without a coach. I was without a job. It was fate.

I returned for the 1973–1974 season to discover that things were beginning to change in college basketball. The game was at the beginning of a period of growth that would become an explosion in just a few years. By the 1980s, college basketball would invade the consciousness of the national sports fan like never before and take its place among the most avidly watched recreations in the country. And eastern college basketball would reach heights it had not experienced since the heyday of Madison Square Garden as the mecca of basketball with the intracity rivalries among CCNY, NYU, Long Island University, Manhattan, Fordham, and St. John's back in the 1940s.

I found that the role of the coach had changed dramatically. In my first tour, and going back to the days of Joe Lapchick, it was a six-month job, October through March. Now it had become a year-round job. In the old days, one guy could run the whole ship, do the recruiting, take care of the academic stuff, whatever had to be done. Now, you have three or four assistants and you have the use of video tape for scouting purposes. In the old days, we would be fortunate to scout a future opponent once. Now, I'll see a team fifteen or twenty times on tape.

Coaching is more sophisticated these days. I don't know if it's any more thorough. In the old days, you were a coach first and a teacher second. Today, coaches are merchandising themselves. They are public relations executives, salesmen, politicians, marketing experts. Coaches are getting endorsements, doing commercials. They have become celebrities.

I even got my own television show and a five-minute, pre-game radio show. Can you imagine that, after 37 years? I never had that before. Now, I do a weekly show on cable television for the Madison Square Garden network, for Bob Gutkowski and Marty Brooks, with Bruce Beck as my co-host. And I have a five-minute radio show for CBS, which carries our games, with Dave Halberstam doing play-by-play and Ed Ingels providing the color. For that I have George Smith to thank. He's my producer. How about that, my producer?

In the old days, you would coach two sports. Today, you have all these assistants. But the pressure was not there like it is today.

When I returned, I found a proliferation of great young college coaches throughout the country and fierce competition for the services of a seemingly unending supply of high school talent. Kids were getting bigger, faster, stronger. They were shooting better than ever, handling the ball better than ever. They were accomplishing things on the basketball court many of us never dreamed possible.

Many things contributed to this college basketball explosion, but two important things stand out in my mind: the involvement of the television networks and the foresight of three men: Dave Gavitt of Providence, Frank Rienzo of Georgetown, and St. John's own Jack Kaiser.

Television has done a tremendous job in bringing our game before the American public, and in so doing, it has even helped infuse new blood into the game. Kids in all corners of the country can now watch the good college players and the pros on television and learn from them, emulate them, and exceed them in ability. Kids from the Midwest become great shooters because every driveway has a basket. They watch the great ones shoot, then they go outside and imitate them for hours.

In the East, you get better ballhandlers because the game is played outside, in playgrounds, on blacktops, and all kinds of surfaces. Also in the East, you could always find enough guys for a pickup game, so city kids seem to have more game smarts. But in the rural areas, kids couldn't always get enough players for a game, so they just shot and shot for hours on end. That probably explains why, in general, kids from small, rural areas are better shooters, but kids from the inner cities are better playmakers and have more game savvy.

The television networks (and I include cable television in this) have become the watchdogs of college basketball, acting as matchmakers, which I believe has had a positive effect on the game. In the old days, you would make your own schedule and pick your spots. You might play six or seven "gimmes" to open the season, so-called easy teams or smaller schools that you knew you could beat. The idea was to boost the confidence of your own team and fatten your record. In the case of St. John's, we would usually be 6–0 or 7–0 before we had to play our first game in Madison Square Garden against a formidable opponent. A school no longer can do that. Today, you might even open your season against a DePaul, a North Carolina or a Kansas, each a basketball power.

Why? Dollars. Let's not kid ourselves. For the money it's putting out to carry college basketball, television wants to be sure it has good attractions that can get ratings. You can't blame the networks. So the networks force you to play good teams because they want good games and intersectional rivalries in exchange for their money and their coverage. If a school wants the television revenue, it has no choice but to play tough teams. All of that is to the benefit of the fan.

The emergence of eastern college basketball can be traced to a summer afternoon in 1979. Jack Kaiser, who had become the athletic director at St. John's, asked me to join him for lunch with Frank Rienzo, the AD at Georgetown, and Dave Gavitt, the AD at Providence College. Over lunch, they discussed the formation of a league of eastern colleges to be called "The Big East." It would involve playing a home-and-home series with each other team in the league, then culminate in a postseason tournament, the winner automatically qualifying for the NCAA postseason championship tournament.

As originally conceived, the Big East was to be an eight-team league comprised of Georgetown, St. John's, Seton Hall, Connecticut, Syracuse, Providence, Holy Cross, and Rutgers. But Holy Cross and Rutgers refused to join, a decision I think they regret today. That's when we picked up Boston College, Villanova and Pittsburgh and it became a nine-team league.

At first, I was vehemently opposed to the idea. Why? For a very selfish reason. As a coach, I was being over-protective. I was secure. Every year, we had gone to a post-season tournament, anyway. What did I need a league for? Why did I need that kind of competition? We played every one of those teams once a year, anyway. Now, we were going to have to play them twice a year, home and home. I was being selfish. I was concerned about myself. What was I going to get out of it?

I presented my objections and they listened, but they went ahead with the league despite my doubts. I'm glad they did. I'm happy to say now that they were right and I was wrong. The Big East has been an unbelievable boon for eastern college basketball, for the school and for the fan. For that, you can credit the foresight of those three men—Jack Kaiser, Frank Rienzo and Dave Gavitt.

True, the competition in our league is fierce, the pressure is intense. But it has brought back eastern college basketball to a position where the Big East can rival any league in the country. We happen to think it's equal to, or better than, any league in the country. In the space of three years, Big East teams won two national championships— Georgetown in 1983 and Villanova in 1985. In the 1985 tournament, three of the four teams in the Final Four were Big East teams and the championship game was played between two teams from our league, Villanova beating Georgetown.

The Big East has also meant more revenue for the schools. We had come a long way in just a few years. I can remember the days when we would draw 2,000–3,000 people in Alumni Hall for a game against Georgetown. Now, we play our Georgetown and Syracuse games in Madison

Square Garden and we sell out the place. And the post-season tournament is a sellout every year.

Until the Big East came along, the most money we ever made at St. John's in any one season was $400,000. Today, we can make $1 million to $1.5 million in a year if we have a successful season. For those who are opposed to college athletics, who think they are too high-powered, too professionalized, there is a ready answer. St. John's is the largest Catholic university in the country with 19,000 full-time students and the money we make from basketball is used to support the twenty-three men's and women's varsity sports that do not generate revenue.

There still is some criticism of the postseason tournament setup and not all of it is without justification. Some say it's not fair to have a postseason tournament in the Big East, that it makes the regular season championship meaningless. There may be some validity to that criticism, but on the other hand, the tournament prepares you for the NCAA tournament. It sharpens you up for the grind that is to come; it prepares you, but it can wear you out, too.

A couple of years ago, we had a great team with Walter Berry, Ron Rowan, and Mark Jackson. We won the Big East tournament, but after that we were so fatigued, we were knocked out early in the NCAAs.

Another criticism is that it's unfair to have to go through a regular season of sixteen games and then to have a tournament. I see nothing wrong with that. It gives a team a second chance. A team might have lost a key player to illness or injury during the season, so it has another chance in the tournament. You've knocked your heads together all year, then you have to do it again. Why? Again, dollars. That's the bottom line, let's not kid ourselves. For four days, we sell out Madison Square Garden. You're talking about whacking up a million dollars or more among the nine teams in the league and that's what it's all about.

Critics of the NCAA tournament say sixty-four teams in the field are too many. It's unwieldy and there are teams in the tournament that obviously don't belong, that have very little, if any, chance of winning. Also, the critics say, it puts too high a premium on depth and strength, which is unfair to the smaller schools. I don't buy it. Just getting into the tournament is enough of an achievement for the smaller schools. And if they knock off one of the bigger schools, that's a feather in their cap. The tournament is a fair test. If you win the NCAA championship, there is no doubt you have earned it.

There's nothing wrong with having sixty-four teams in the tournament. It gets everybody involved. It has helped make a regional sport national in scope. It has helped create the mystique in the tournament, much like the Super Bowl, only better. There's a game every weekend, lose and out. It generates excitement and attention. For three weeks in March, the country is wild with basketball mania.

Some little school in the Northwest or the Northeast has a chance to win. Overnight, you become a somebody.

Another criticism is putting a team from the East, like St. John's, in the West region. I don't see anything wrong with that, either. It's much better than having a team playing in its own backyard, especially on its home court, like Syracuse and DePaul. I'm not picking on Syracuse playing in the Carrier Dome or DePaul playing in the Rosemont Horizon. That's done because those arenas are large and they can sell more tickets and generate more revenue. That's fine, but it's not fair for Syracuse to play a tournament game in the Carrier Dome and DePaul to play a tournament game in the Rosemont Horizon because that's where they play their home games. Again, I'm not picking on Syracuse and

DePaul, but I don't think that's fair. It's too great an advantage for a tournament of such importance. We have traveled more than any other team in the country, but I'm not complaining. It's an honor and a thrill to compete in the NCAA tournament.

I can understand why they want to have some games in big arenas, but I don't like it. Basketball was not meant to be played in front of crowds of 50,000 or 60,000. It's not like soccer. The people can't see the game. That's one of the reasons I have campaigned for the use of a red, white, and blue basketball, like we used in the old American Basketball Association. It's easier to see than the brownish-orange ball we're using.

The bottom line, of course, is dollars. And if you get into the NCAA tournament, that means revenue for the school and in some schools, that revenue translates into better professors, better labs, better facilities. In our case, it supports our other varsity teams. It also helps with recruiting because the television exposure makes your school and your program better known to a greater number of people. In the past, St. John's always was a neighborhood school—about 95 percent of our players came from the New York area. Now, because of playing in the NCAA tournament and the national television exposure, we have been able to recruit players from all over the country.

There is a negative side to all this, however. It probably has shortened the careers of coaches because the pressure to win is greater now than it's ever been. In the old days, a school would be willing to stay with a coach for a longer period of time. He would have three or four years to grow with his team and improve along with the team. Today, because of the money that's at stake, the pressure to win right away is much greater, so a school won't stay with a coach for very long. You find yourself coaching with your bags packed. If a coach doesn't win in two years, he's gone and another coach is brought in to take his place.

I feel blessed to have survived in college coaching for so long, to have been associated with such a great university and to have coached some great players.

People are always asking me which has been my favorite team. That's a hard question to answer because your favorite team may not necessarily have been your best team. People would say, "Louie, you did a good coaching job," because you may have won twenty-five or twenty-six games. But some of your best coaching jobs are with teams whose record might not show it. You have to do a good coaching job just to keep them going, to keep the ship afloat. I had a team one year that finished 18-12, but they were a great bunch of kids. They kept losing games by one, two and three points, but they always came back. Those are the teams you really appreciate.

Then there was our 1980–1981 team. We called them "The Gang That Couldn't Shoot Straight," for obvious reasons. They were a good bunch of kids, good athletes. They could handle the ball, play defense, rebound. But they just couldn't shoot. I thought it was just nervousness. I tried everything to help them relax—played music in the dressing room before practice, during practice, after practice; I tried giving them days off, tried telling them jokes, tried speaking softly and soothingly to them. Nothing worked. We even had t-shirts made up for the players that said, "The Gang That Couldn't Shoot Straight."

We played Oregon State on national television on a Saturday afternoon in the Nassau Coliseum. They were the number one team in the country at that time. And we were terrible. We went 18 minutes without scoring at one stretch. We couldn't even hit a foul shot. We couldn't find anything.

Missing layups. Balls were bouncing off the rim. I was so frustrated.

The next week, we go up to play Providence and we go eight minutes without scoring. The following Thursday, we go four minutes without scoring against Seton Hall. There was nothing we could do, they were just lousy shooters.

At the end of the season, Oregon State gets an NCAA bid, and I run into the Oregon State coach, Ralph Miller, who just was elected to the Hall of Fame.

"You know, Lou," Miller said. "After we played you, my club was never the same. We just couldn't make a shot to save ourselves."

I guess whatever we had, we gave it to them.

I'd be remiss if I didn't single out the 1984–1985 club that went to the Final Four. That was the team that had Chris Mullin, Bill Wennington, Willie Glass, Mike Moses, Ron Rowan, Walter Berry, Mark Jackson, Ron Stewart, Terry Bross, Steve Shurina and Shelton Jones. Anybody could have coached that club. It was a very coachable group and very talented. I'd have to say that was my best team because they loved basketball so much.

With them, practice was an event. Mullin would never take a shot in practice. He'd just concentrate on passing and moving the ball, making plays for others.

One day I chased them out of the gym. "Get out of here, dammit," I shouted. "Get lost. Go home." I was really ticked off at them. They were terrible during practice. Their attitude, their performance. Terrible. Like they didn't care. So I chased them out and went upstairs to my office. About a half hour later, somebody came to my office and said, "Hey, Coach, take a look at what's going on in the gym."

I went down and there was the team practicing by

themselves. That shows the kind of club that was, the dedication, the desire. That's why I say that team was special and that's why they were so successful.

We went to the NCAAs and were placed in the West region and had to play in Salt Lake City. We advanced to Denver, where we won our region and that sent us to the Final Four in Lexington, Ky. There were three Big East teams in the Final Four that year—Georgetown, Villanova, and St. John's.

We drew Georgetown in the semifinals and they beat us. We played them four times that season and we beat them only once. I thought Georgetown was the best team in the country, but they lost in the finals to Villanova in one of the biggest upsets in NCAA history. Villanova just shot the eyes out of the basket and played smart basketball.

Still, there is no doubt in my mind that Georgetown was a better team. We beat Villanova three times in three games that season and Georgetown beat us three out of four. If Georgetown played Villanova ten times, I'm convinced it would have won nine times, they were that good. That one other time just happened to come in the national championship game. Just one of those things, but Villanova deserved it that night. It just goes to show what I have been saying about the NCAA tournament. Any team can win. Any team has a chance to be somebody.

Villanova's victory proved that anything can happen in the game of basketball: Anything is possible, especially when you're dealing with college kids, twenty-one and twenty-two years old and younger.

I was disappointed we didn't win the national championship that year. It was tough to swallow because we had such a good team. But we lost to a great team in Georgetown. I was mostly disappointed for our fans, who supported us so loyally, and for our kids, who worked so hard and had such great expectations. But it wasn't the end of the world and they had nothing to be ashamed of. It was a great experience and they got to the Final Four. That's something to be proud of. I was proud of them and I told them so.

NINE

The Sweater

I will admit I never considered myself the picture of sartorial splendor. I'll never win an award as the best-dressed coach in basketball or get mentioned on anyone's Ten Best-Dressed List. I mean, I'm not Chuck Daly or Mike Fratello or Pat Riley when it comes to clothes.

Clothes never have been very important to me. Don't get me wrong, I like wearing nice clothes and I try to dress appropriately for the occasion and to always look neat. It's just that I never have made a fetish about clothes, no $1,000 suits, no tailor-made, high fashion design for me. Mention Fendi, Giorgio Armani, or Oleg Cassini to me and I may think you're talking about the front line of the Italian National basketball team.

What I'm trying to say is that there are tailor-made people and off-the-rack people. I'm definitely off the rack. Maybe it's because I don't have the body for clothes. Never did. In my mind, I am six feet, two inches tall and stylishly slim. I look like a cross between Cary Grant and Paul Newman in my mind. In real life, I am too short, I have a little pot belly, and my shoulders slump. I don't think Gentleman's Quarterly ever is going to hire me to model the latest fashions. So I wear what suits me and what is comfortable and I'll let those other guys make the Best-Dressed Lists.

If a guy wants to get dressed to the nines to coach a basketball game, that's his privilege. It doesn't make him a better, or a worse, coach.

We once played against Seton Hall, coached by Billy Raftery. Billy showed up wearing a light blue, three-piece suit. He looked like Billy Daniels.

"Where the hell do you think we're playing this game," I asked him. "In the Fountainbleu?"

Actually, there was a time when I was younger that I used to be very clothes conscious and thought I was very stylish. I even used to wear garters to hold up my socks. There was a time, believe it or not, when garters were very much the "in" thing in men's fashion.

People used to kid me about my garters, and I'd always tell them, "Show me a man with garters, and I'll show you a man with class."

I stopped wearing garters just about the time I stopped wearing shorts, when Buck Freeman made fun of my legs that time at Clair Bee's camp. I haven't worn shorts since. These legs have not seen the sun in more than thirty years.

Although I'm no longer a clothes person, I think I am safe in saying a piece of my clothing has received more attention in the sports world than any other piece of clothing I can think of. Me. Lou Carnesecca, a guy whose wardrobe can best be described as Early Austerity.

Not only that, the garment to which I refer is now in the Basketball Hall of Fame in Springfield, Massachusetts. They didn't ask Pat Riley for his tie or Mike Fratello for his vest or Chuck Daly for one of his Italian silk suits. No. But they came to me and requested a piece of my clothing. Eat your heart out, Cesar Romero.

Of course, I'm referring to a garment that came to be quite familiarly known as The Sweater. Or Looie's Sweater. Or Lou Carnesecca's Lucky Sweater. Maybe you remember hearing about it or even seeing it. If you ever saw it, it's a cinch you haven't forgotten it. You couldn't possibly forget it, any more than you can forget a bad dream.

Before I tell you about The Sweater—how, where and from whom I got it, how it got to be so famous, and what it meant to me—let me digress for a moment to discuss a subject that is very controversial, very serious, and one of my pet peeves. Clothing. More specifically, the clothes worn by basketball coaches.

Let me put this in the form of a question: Why the hell do basketball coaches have to wear suits, shirts, and ties on the bench during a game? Who ever made this a rule? Who set the standard? Do they give points for neatness? Are you susceptible to a technical foul if you're a slob?

I think it's absolutely ridiculous. I mean, we're not going to the Inaugural Ball, we're going to work. This is not a formal occasion. Would it help my team if I wore a tuxedo?

No other sport requires the coach, or manager, to wear a suit and a tie. Have you noticed the attire of football coaches on the sidelines? Most of them look like they're going out jogging, or they are about to tee off on the first hole. But nobody says anything about it. Tom Landry of the Dallas Cowboys is about the only coach who gets dressed up like he's going on his first date. Landry, in fact, gets dressed from head to toe. He always wears a suit, or a sports coat, and a tie. And he always wears a hat, and I know why. It's because he's losing his hair.

Most of the other coaches in the NFL look like they're relaxing in their backyards. Bill Parcells of the Giants usually will wear a jogging suit. Don Shula of the Dolphins wears slacks and a short-sleeve sports shirt. I think that's very sensible.

Baseball managers go the other way. They wear the same uniform as their players, which I think is also ridiculous. But at least it's more practical than wearing a three-piece suit.

Connie Mack of the old Philadelphia Athletics and Burt Shotton of the Brooklyn Dodgers were the only baseball managers I can think of who did not wear a uniform. Mack wore a three-piece suit with a starched collar and tie and he always wore a straw hat. But he didn't have to hit. Shotton was dressed a little more practically. He wore a Dodgers warmup jacket over his shirt and tie, but he had his street trousers on. As a result, neither Mack nor Shotton was permitted to go onto the field. When they wanted to pass along instructions, they let one of their coaches, dressed in a uniform, be the messenger.

I am told that the reason baseball managers were required to wear uniforms is that they used to coach on the lines and if you're in the coaching box, in full view of the fans and part of the action, you should be dressed like the members of the team for uniformity. But it's been years since a baseball manager has coached on the lines. The only time a baseball manager appears on the field now is to go to the mound to talk to the pitcher or to go out and argue with an umpire. I guess you wouldn't want to be overdressed when you argue with an umpire.

You watch, in about ten years or less, the manager won't even have to leave the dugout to talk to his pitcher or remove him from a game. He'll have a little microphone in the dugout and the pitcher will have a receiver in his ear, or on his uniform, and the manager will communicate with him without ever leaving his seat. He won't have to be in uniform to do that. But I don't see any solution for going out on the field to argue with an umpire. That's something you want to do in person and face-to-face. Can you picture Billy Martin, dressed in a three-piece suit, running out to kick dirt on an umpire? So, I guess for practical purposes, baseball managers and college baseball coaches will just continue to wear uniforms.

But why in the name of James Naismith do basketball coaches have to wear suits and ties?

I think the answer to that is because it's always been done. And those of us in sports get bogged down in tradition. Too often the answer to why we do certain things is that's the way we always have done them.

Why not be comfortable? I'd like to wear slacks, an open-neck shirt, maybe a sweater with the school's logo or its name on it. Or even a jogging suit in the school's colors and with the school's name on it. George Raveling of USC wears a jogging suit when he coaches. That to me is more practical and more comfortable. No, we are expected to get dressed up like we're going to the Senior Prom. So you wear a nice, expensive suit and the next thing you know you're kneeling, stretching, jumping, and sweating and you've ruined your suit.

I once ruined a nice, brand new blue serge suit at Madison Square Garden. I caught the sleeve on a nail and tore the sleeve. It ruined the suit. And the Garden never even offered to pay to replace the suit or repair it, those bums. It was a beautiful suit, too. That's why I don't keep my jacket on any more when I'm coaching. It's too restricting.

How many times have I taken off my jacket and thrown it on the floor when I didn't like a referee's call? I ruined a lot of jackets that way. I have even lost things that came flying out of my pockets when I threw my jacket. I've lost glasses, pens, even change. I must have lost thousands of dollars because I threw my jacket on the floor.

All right, hundreds of dollars. Would you believe a buck twenty?

That's why I don't keep my jacket on any more when I'm coaching. I don't have many superstitions but one is the way I dress for a game. I always wear brown pants, a blue button-down shirt and tie. I usually wear a camel's hair jacket to go with it, but I never wear the jacket on the bench; I leave it in the locker room. I don't want to risk tearing a camel's hair jacket.

Most of the time the tie comes off or the knot comes loose and is hanging down around my chest. You can usually tell how tough the game is by the position of the knot in my tie. The tougher the game, the lower the knot.

After a game, I'm soaked with perspiration. I'm sweating, I'm tired. I have to take a shower. I play the entire game, both ends of the floor. I throw every pass, make every play, shoot every basket, block every shot, make every call. I do that just to help the officials do their job, you understand. Unfortunately, they don't listen to me. I go through the whole thing. I'm running up and down along the sidelines. I'm kneeling in supplication. I'm stretching, bending, jumping. By the time the game ends, I'm wringing wet and I'm exhausted. That's why I'd like to wear a pair of slacks and a sports shirt. And, of course, a sweater.

I promised to tell you the story of The Sweater. It all happened in the 1984–1985 season. I had been entertaining a few coaches from Italy who came to St. John's to spend a few weeks to study and learn the game of basketball from an American coach's point of view. As their visit was coming to an end, Massimo Tracuzzi, the coach of the Italian women's team, came into my office and told me, in Italian, that he wanted to give me a present in appreciation for the hospitality we had shown him at St. John's. I thanked him profusely, also in Italian, and took the package he handed me without opening it. It wasn't until much later, after they had left, that I opened the package. I couldn't believe my eyes.

In the package were two of the ugliest sweaters I had ever seen. One was uglier than the other. They looked like some kindergarten kid's finger painting. One of the sweaters—the one that got all the attention—had a big chevron on the front. If you remember the logo of the old Chevron gas stations, that's what it looks like. The design wasn't so bad. It was the colors that made it so, uh, shall we say unusual. It has a blue chevron and a red chevron against a background of burnt siena. Some combination. Made me think it was designed by Helen Keller. I just took the two sweaters and tossed them in the closet and forgot about them. I never intended to wear them.

That was in October. Later that season, in January, we were scheduled to go to Pittsburgh and I was feeling lousy. I had a cold that I just couldn't shake, sore throat, hacking cough, and all. Mary said to me, "Listen, you've got a cold and you're going into all these drafty gyms. You're going to wind up with pneumonia. Why don't you take a sweater and wear it during the game to keep from getting a chill?"

I always have listened to Mary. She's the sensible and practical one in the family, so I took her advice. I put my hand in the closet in my office to grab a sweater and it was one of the ugly sweaters from Italy.

We go to Pittsburgh and everybody starts getting on me about the ugly sweater I'm wearing—the players, my coaches, the press, everybody.

"Hey," I told them. "Don't go knocking this sweater. It was given to me as a gift by the coach of the Italian women's National team and he said it has special magical powers. This is my lucky sweater."

Sure enough, we beat Pittsburgh by one point in one of the most exciting games of the year and, after the game, in the postgame press conference, the writers kept asking me about my lucky sweater.

"Was it the sweater that did it?" they asked.

"Yeah," I said, never one to fail to see a good story. "I told you this was a lucky sweater."

And the next day, in all the papers, all the stories were about my lucky sweater. I'm a little superstitious anyway, but now I'm trapped. I have to wear the sweater at the next game whether I want to or not. Everybody's looking for it. My coaches are looking for it. The press is looking for it. My players are looking for it. And wouldn't you know it, we suddenly go on a winning streak and the more we win, the more stories are being written about the sweater and the more people are looking for it. Now, they're not only writing about it, they're talking about it on the radio, showing it on television. That sweater was becoming a celebrity.

We'd go on a road trip and I'd go down to the hotel lobby during the day, or down to the coffee shop in the morning for breakfast without the sweater, just a shirt and tie. And the kids would look at me and I could tell they were thinking, "Is he going to wear the sweater tonight at the game?"

I'm not one to fly in the face of superstition or challenge a higher authority. As long as we kept winning, I kept wearing the sweater. But let me tell you, it was getting to be a problem. Mary had to wash it because it would get all sweaty, but I couldn't send it out to the cleaners for fear I wouldn't get it back in time for the next game. The sweater was pure wool and the more she washed it, the more it shrank. It kept getting smaller and smaller.

Another thing, as the season wore on the weather warmed up and there were times when I was dying in that sweater. It was hot and it itched and it kept getting smaller and smaller, but I didn't dare take it off as long as we were winning. Everybody was involved in it, even the kids. Hey, if a little discomfort is the price you have to pay for victory, I'll pay it any time.

The Sweater also resulted in a couple of funny incidents before two games with Georgetown. John Thompson, Georgetown's coach, and I have enjoyed a friendly rivalry through the years. I like John and I especially like to match wits with him, not only on the basketball court but in the area of promotions and publicity.

My sweater had been getting so much attention and we were playing Georgetown in Madison Square Garden. Everybody's talking about The Sweater, but John hadn't said anything about it. I thought that was kind of unusual, but I let it pass figuring he was too wrapped up in the game. I was wrong.

I have a pregame ritual that I picked up from Joe Lapchick. I like to visit with the opposing coach before the game. Now, I walk over to Big John, who's standing there nice and neat in his suit and tie. I never suspected a thing. Just as I get up to him, he opens his jacket like Superman taking off his shirt and under the jacket he's wearing a multicolored sweater that's even uglier than mine.

Naturally, the place went wild. He had tipped off the gag to the television people, so they got it on camera. I couldn't resist. I just broke up laughing. He had me, but good. I didn't mind him upstaging me with the sweater, the big sonofagun, but he won the ball game, too. That's what really hurt.

If you know me, you know I wasn't going to just drop it there, let him get the upper hand on me and let it go at that. I had to cook up something to get even with him. I thought and thought, and finally I had it.

John always has a towel draped across his shoulder when he's on the bench. That gave me an idea to get even with him for his sweater trick. My opportunity came a few weeks later, in the Big East tournament. This was perfect.

Before the game, I let John walk out on the floor first. Then I came out. What I had done was get somebody to sew a bunch of towels together to make one long one, about forty or fifty feet long, and I draped it over my shoulder. I walked out on the floor, right up to John with the towel dragging on the floor behind me. Everybody cracked up, none more than John Thompson, himself. And I had scored my revenge.

I think that's the kind of thing you have to do in sports. It was just good fun and you have to have fun. It's only a game (sure, it is, and the Grand Canyon is only a hole in the ground). But people remember those things. Maybe they remember them long after the victories and defeats and I think that's as it should be.

To this day, people still remember the sweater. If I walk down the street or meet people for the first time, four out of five people I meet will say, "Hey, Lou, where's your sweater?"

The sweater is a part of history now in the Basketball Hall of Fame in Springfield. You can see it if you visit the Hall of Fame, if you have the stomach for it. I was only too happy to part with it when they asked for it. I was very flattered. It's there for everybody to see, a little smaller than it was originally, but just as ugly.

I don't know of another article of clothing that was so involved with a sport, or a team, like this sweater. The whole thing was simply unbelievable. A lot of people thought I was getting paid from a sweater company to wear it or that I would end up with a sweater commercial. Not at all. Nobody would make up a sweater that ugly and advertise it. I never made a cent out of that sweater. Honest. But maybe that's the way it ought to be. We had a lot of fun with it.

People related to it. And it certainly didn't hurt St. John's, the Big East, or the game of basketball.

It's unbelievable how it caught on. Here I thought I was a great coach, a great tactician, a great strategist. No, The Sweater won all those games.

Enes, me and Mary with His Holiness, Pope Paul VI. He asked me a question in English, and I was so flustered I answered in Italian.

That's Mom on the right with her sister, my Zia Ida—two of the three Andrews Sisters.

Big game hunters, Pop and his pals after a hunting trip in upstate New York. That's Pop on the far right in the leather jacket and the cool hat.

Even at the age of 19, I was partial to ugly sweaters. I was better looking then, and the guy did a hell of a job with the camera. (CAROLA STUDIO, NY)

Here I am with some friends from the coaching fraternity. On the left is Utah Jazz coach Frank Layden, about 100 pounds ago. On the right is my former assistant John Kresse. I'm so proud of his success at the College of Charleston. On the far right is my pal Bernie (Red) Sarachek. (WILLIAM PICCIONE)

"Hizzoner," the Governor of New York, Mario M. Cuomo, my old center fielder. He always had good hands.

A family portrait. Enes, Mary, me
and Missy.

My daughter's wedding, 1979. Left to right: me, Mary, Mary's mother
Assunta Chiesa, my daughter Enes, my son-in-law Jerry Frunzi, and my
parents Alfred and Adele Carnesecca. The wedding ceremony was held in the
chapel on St. John's University campus.

Winning the Joe Lapchick Tournament championship. Me, co-captain Trevor Jackson, Joe's daughter Barbara Lapchick, and co-captain David Russell.

At left is my old classmate, Hall of Famer, Dick McGuire. He was a magician with a basketball in his hands. At right, the late Lloyd (Sonny) Dove. It broke me up when he was killed in an accident.

That's little Gene Leone and "The Big Indian," Joe Lapchick. Gene had a good fork and he was a wonderful host at his famous restaurant, Mamma Leone's.

That's me making a point at a clinic in the old country, Italy. (ANGELO SBARAGA, ROME)

Me and The Coach, Frank McGuire, *top left*. He could have run for Mayor of New York and won in a landslide. (CHUCK BENSON)

Enjoying a laugh, *top right*, with my friend Dean-O, I mean, Dean Smith. (GEORGE KALINSKY, MAJOR LEAGUE GRAPHICS)

My partner and friend Red Sarachek and me, *left*. Those two bugles could make some set of bookends. (METRO SPORTS TEAM PIX)

'Do it this way . . . and if that doesn't work, do it that way.'' (MIKE MARTEN)

I guess things weren't going well for us when this picture was taken.

Opposite: one of my referee pals asked me for directions and here I'm patiently and calmly telling him where to go. (STEVE PARKER)

Seniors Mark Jackson, Willie Glass and John Hempel after we won our final home game in the 1986–87 season.

Another Joe Lapchick Tournament championship. Chris Mullin, me, Joe's son Richard Lapchick, Joe's widow Barbara Lapchick, Ron Stewart and Bill Wennington.

The only way to travel—on the shoulders of your players after a big victory.
(DON FANELL)

That's the Big East championship trophy. Ron Stewart, Chris Mullin and Bill Wennington help me carry it. (MIKE MARTEN)

Here I am during an audition for the role of Quasimodo in *The Hunchback of Notre Dame*. (BOB OLEN, *NEW YORK POST*)

I second the motion.
(H. SCHWARTZMAS)

The real coach, The Sweater. It was much bigger when I wore it than when the Hall of Fame in Springfield, Massachusetts got it.
(MARK M. MURRAY)

You know we're winning because my tie is almost in my collar.

I'm surrounded by McGuires: Dick on the left and his brother, Al, on the right. Behind us is Kevin Loughery, one of the original gym rats and a great player. He's another one they said couldn't run and couldn't jump, but he played eleven season in the NBA and was a great coach too. (CYRIL MORRIS)

The Brothers McGuire, then and now, when they were inducted into the St. John's Hall of Fame. (CYRIL MORRIS)

Willis Reed showed me something when he came to St. John's as an unpaid assistant —he even paid his own travel expenses. I'm rooting for him to do a great job as coach of the New Jersey Nets. I know he will.

TEN

Game Day and Recruiting

Game Day is when it all comes together, all the hard work, all the preparation, all the planning, all the practice. This is what you work for, from the first day you assemble your team. Even before then. When you go out and recruit those high school kids. This is the culmination of all the hours of practice, the hours of looking at tapes of your opponent, the mapping of strategy with your coaches.

You find yourself running through a gamut of emotions on Game Day. Fear. Anxiety. Anticipation. Exhilaration. Worry. Is your team prepared? Is it properly motivated and ready to play? Did you cover everything? Will the opposing coach come up with something new that you didn't cover, that you didn't see in the films? So many things go through your mind on Game Day. There are so many details to think about. But there is one thing that is always true. By the time Game Day has rolled around, whatever you have had to cover has been covered. Your work as a coach is done. From that point on, it's pretty much up to the players to win the game or lose it.

Our routine on Game Day is usually about the same. If it's a home game, I'll get to my office about eight or nine in the morning, lock myself up and just gather my thoughts. I try to get some of my paper work done. I'll hang around the school all day. I don't go home. I just make sure everything is ready for the game.

At about three or three-thirty in the afternoon, the whole team and all the coaches go to Dante's Restaurant on Union Turnpike where Carmen Piacentini, the owner, provides us with a pregame meal. He'll usually serve steak, which is high in protein, and pasta, which is high in carbohydrates. The kids eat. I can't eat before a game. I can't keep it down. So I sit back and I make some notes and go over the scouting report with my assistants, Brian Mahoney, Ron Rutledge and Al LoBalbo.

After dinner, we go back to the school and we have meetings. We show the kids video tape of our opponent. What kind of offense and defense do they play? What are their individual characteristics?

That will take about twenty minutes to a half hour. Then they go out and relax for awhile. If there's a women's game being played in the gym, which there usually is on game days, our players will watch that game. Then they'll come back and we go over the scouting report with them. I try not to take any telephone calls on Game Day, unless it's an emergency. I don't want to have any unnecessary distractions.

Time has become very precious. I have my television show once a week. I have a five-minute pregame radio show. I'm on the Board of Directors of the National Association of Basketball Coaches. There's hardly any time to be a coach.

When we have a road game, it doesn't differ greatly, except that we get to the city where we're playing the night before the game so that we get a good night's sleep. On the night we travel (either by bus or by plane if it's a long trip) we'll go to Dante's before we leave to be sure the kids get a good meal. After a good night's sleep, we'll meet at about ten o'clock the next morning for brunch. Then we go to the gym to shoot around so the kids can loosen up. At 3:30 or four, depending on the time of the game, we'll have our pregame meal. Usually, the hotel where we're staying will provide a private room for our pregame meal and another room where we can have our meetings and watch our films.

After dinner, we'll gather and go over the films and the scouting report. We'll go over everything three or four times to be sure everybody understands what we're going to do and what we think the other team is going to do.

After the game, I'll get together with my coaches, not the players. If we're home, we'll go over to Dante's. If we're on the road, we'll just meet in the hotel and go over what happened in the game.

Wherever we are, we try to get together in private. I think that's very important. That's why our St. John's family has always been so strong. It's part of the coaching philosophy. We talk things out, what went wrong, what we could have done here, what we should have done there. We have disagreements. We have our differences. I wouldn't want yes men for assistant coaches. But it never gets nasty, and we all come out with one thought. I think disagreements are good. But I believe in keeping it to ourselves, not airing our dirty linen in public. That's why we get together in private. Their wives are there, priests are there, but no outsiders. That's important because if guys go different ways, you never know who you're talking to, or who will overhear what you say. You might say something, some stranger will hear it, and blow it out of proportion.

Let's say you disagree with my philosophy. "He should have done this." The next thing you know, there's a story that coach A is second-guessing coach B. I want to avoid that.

I tell my kids the same thing. Don't go places where there are strangers. You might miss a layup and go someplace and have a beer and the next thing somebody is calling you a drunkard. I tell them to go with their friends. The idea is to air your differences in private with your loved ones, with your people.

Normally, I don't have trouble sleeping the night before the game. The night of the game, I can't sleep. Win or lose, I'm too wound up. My mind is racing. I'm playing every play all over.

Actually, the bigger the game the less the pressure. It's the games that you're supposed to win that you die. I worry about every little thing that can go wrong. The big games, against the good teams, I don't worry about that much because I know the kids are going to be up for those games. My biggest fear is when we play the so-called schlunks, the games you figure to win. That's when as a coach I have to work a little harder on motivation.

How do you motivate a kid? It varies, depending on the kid. What kind of kid is he? What kind of motivation does he need? What makes this kid tick? I try to find that out. A lot of things can motivate people. Money. Fear. Fear of failure, which is probably the greatest driving force of all. I try to always be positive and the thing I try to develop most is pride. Pride in performance. Every time you step on that court, you want to do your best.

How many times have I heard a kid say, "I wasn't up for the ballgame." That's a lot of crap. I never heard a kid say, "Tonight, I'm going to go out there and stink up the joint." Kids don't say that. When a kid says he wasn't up for the game after the game, that's an alibi. I don't want to hear that. Give the other guy credit. He was better. I want them to develop pride, that they're performers, they're on stage and to give their best. If you give your best and you get beat, you can live with yourself.

Another alibi. "I was tired." Did you ever see a winning team that was tired? That's an excuse. I have an expression

I like to use that I got from Danny Whelan, who was the trainer for the New York Knicks championship teams. "You're not tired," Danny used to say. "You just need more rest."

Something new has come into play in recent years that comes under the heading of preparation and that is the media attention. We always used to have the press at our games, but not like it has become recently with the boom in college basketball. Especially when you're fortunate to reach the Final Four. It was unbelievable. The kids wouldn't get home until nine or ten o'clock at night. And as a coach you always have to be on call. The press needs to reach you. Newspapers, television, and radio need a story and you have to accommodate them.

I've been around for a long time. I'm used to dealing with the press. I've done it for years and I had a great teacher in dealing with the press, Joe Lapchick. I get criticized, I get misquoted, I get second-guessed. You learn to live with it. You accept it because you're not going to win that battle if you get into a debate with the writers who rip you. I realize, too, that those people have a job to do. They have to get a story and I'll try to help them in any way I can. If they rip me, I can't fight that. My philosophy regarding dealing with the press is that if you take the pats, you have to take the raps. Sometimes the raps are unfair, but that's something you can't control.

I have an obligation and the press has an obligation, to the truth. A reporter has a job to do and I have to furnish him with information, whether I like him or not. I don't have to tell him everything. There are certain things I'm not going to tell him. But I have to recognize that he has a job to do and I also have to recognize my obligation to my university to help get publicity.

I have been very fortunate through the years in my dealings with the press. I have been treated fairly by most members of the media. I would say the negative stuff has been very, very infrequent. But I'm a professional and I have learned how to deal with it.

The kids are a different story. This may be their first experience with this sort of thing.

I try to pass along to my kids my philosophy for dealing with the press. Treat them the way you would like them to treat you. If you do that, you won't have a problem.

The truth is the big thing. If you're truthful to the press and the press is truthful to you, that's all that matters. It's when the press comes with their story all made up in their heads and fits whatever situation is out there to the story, that breeds mistrust. And I have found this to be the pattern in the last six or seven years. I don't know why, whether it's become more competitive because of television, or whether it's because college basketball is getting more publicity than ever before. All I know is that I have seen changes in the attitude of the press.

What concerns me is that because of the great amount of publicity we're getting, with the NCAA tournament and the Big East, the press is treating these college kids like professionals. I'm not talking only about newspapers. The same goes for television commentators. I hear them ripping kids and that's just not fair. A kid misses a layup and he gets ripped. You're dealing with kids who are very frail. These commentators don't know the harm they can do. These kids have girl friends, they have friends, they have parents. These commentators treat these kids like pros because of the mass attention, and most kids are not ready for that. If they were pros, they'd have to take it whether they liked it or not. But they're not pros. They're eighteen, nineteen, and twenty years old and they're vulnerable. They're inexperienced. Many of them are dealing with the press for the first time.

I don't believe in sheltering these kids. I didn't agree with John Wooden when he refused to let Kareem Abdul-Jabbar talk to the press when he was at UCLA. I can understand screening his interviews and budgeting his time, but I think dealing with the press is part of the educational process for a college athlete.

We're supposed to be educators. At St. John's, we send our athletes to a speech teacher, who interviews them, puts the interview on tape, then plays it back so the kid can listen to it. Then the teacher points out the mistakes and together they work on trying to correct those mistakes. If a kid makes a mistake in an interview, it's no different than missing a layup in the game. So what. He made a mistake. He's got to learn. That's part of his education, part of his learning process. If you lock him up and shut him up, he'll never learn. One of these days he's going to have to learn to handle it. The ability to stand up at a press conference in front of a hundred tough, veteran members of the media popping questions at him, how many kids who aren't athletes can do that? How many even get the chance? And the more he does it, the better he'll get at it. He'll learn to say the right thing, not to hurt people. He should be allowed to speak his mind. He'll learn how to handle himself. So what if his grammar isn't good. Neither is mine. So what if he says the wrong thing. Sometimes you're embarrassed by your own children.

That's why I disagreed with Wooden. Shutting a guy up, putting a gag on him is wrong and it's doing a disservice to the kid. It's not preparing him for life after school. As educators, isn't that what we are supposed to be doing?

When we had the Final Four team our kids were constantly being badgered by the press. So what. It was a great learning experience for them. What they learned could never be taught in a classroom.

* * *

Some years ago, I went to Cornwall-on-Hudson, a town in upstate New York, to talk to a kid about coming to St. John's. It isn't often that we recruit out of our immediate area, but this kid, Paul Berwanger, expressed an interest in coming to St. John's and we wanted him. He was all set to go to Boston College, but he didn't want to go. His mother wanted him to go. He wanted to come to St. John's, so he invited us up to talk to his mother.

I made the trip with my assistant, Brian Mahoney. Our plan was to meet with Paul and his mother at his house, tell his mother about the advantages of coming to St. John's, convince her that it was best for her son, and get a commitment that he would be coming to school. As simple as that.

We get there and there's Paul, his mother, and his high school coach. We were welcomed warmly and Mrs. Berwanger had even made coffee for us and on the table she had a plate of delicious-looking apple turnovers, which she served. Such hospitality is always a good sign.

We sit down and Mrs. Berwanger is pouring coffee. I pick up an apple turnover and I say, "Mrs. Berwanger, we're so happy that Paul is thinking of coming to St. John's."

I'm just about to take a bite out of the apple turnover and she shrieks, "What? My son is going to Boston College and you get out of my house right now."

She chased me right out of the house. I didn't even get to eat the apple turnover, and it looked so good.

As we left, I said, "Mrs. Berwanger, let me tell you something. You might send your son to Boston College, but he's not going to stay there."

Sure enough, a year later Paul transferred to St. John's and he became a very productive player for us. He graduated, played in France, and today he's working in law enforcement in Michigan.

There's a point to this story and that is if a kid doesn't want to go to a school, no amount of pressure from his family or his friends is going to force him to go. He may go but he won't stay. Occasionally, you can recruit the parents, but more often than not, it's the kid himself who makes the decision.

The other point is that I don't care how great a coach you may be, how good a strategist and technician, how good an Xs and Os man, all that means nothing if you don't have the talent to execute your plays, your plans, and your theories. Much of the success of a coach depends on what he and his staff do long before game day, even long before the start of practice. And the name of that game is recruiting.

There is no formula for recruiting, no one way you go about getting a kid interested in coming to your school. Each case is different. Most times, the kid recruits himself. By that I mean, he makes up his mind where he wants to go to school, sometimes years before it's time for him to make that decision. And there can be any number of reasons why a kid decides he wants to go to a certain school. He may have watched your games on television; he may have taken a liking to a particular player on your team and has followed him; he may like the color of your uniforms; he may think your cheerleaders are pretty. Maybe he has a friend who goes to the school, or a relative, or an older person in his neighborhood whom he admires.

As I have said, it's usually the kid who makes the decision, but there are times you have to win over the parents. Their main concern is academics and what their son's chances are of getting a degree. That's when I'm happy and proud to tell them that in the past twenty-five years over 86 percent of our kids have graduated.

With the kids, it's a different approach. Their concern is where they are going to play, how much they're going to play and usually my pitch with them is New York City and

St. John's tradition. Madison Square Garden is a big factor for us. It's the mecca of basketball and I let kids know that we play ten to twelve games there every season. We play a great schedule. The opportunity for them is tremendous. If they play for us, they're going to be seen. If they think they have a shot at pro ball, they know the scouts are not going to overlook us.

For some kids, the cultural advantages of playing in New York is important. It's the financial center of the world, the media capital of the world, the cultural center of the world. The museums, the theaters. Anything you want is right here, I tell them. And the opportunity is there for them. As Frank Sinatra says in the song, "If you can make it here, you can make it anywhere."

I also point out to the local kids that if they stay at home, they get to play in front of their friends and family. That's a big thing for a lot of kids. Like I say, the kid recruits himself. He knows if he wants to stay in New York (if he's local) or come to New York (if he's from out of town). And the local kids know if they want to get out of the city. If that's what they want, there's no way I'm going to get them. Kenny Smith and Pearl Washington are two who come to mind that fall into that category. We talked to both of them, but they had their minds made up they wanted to go out of town. So Kenny went to North Carolina and Pearl wound up in Syracuse, and, thank God, we got Mark Jackson.

I've always felt our best bet was to recruit in the New York area. We know the kids. We know their coaches. We've seen these kids play in high school, we've watched them grow up. Except for certain cases, most of our kids come from right here in our backyard.

There's so much basketball talent in the New York area. You have only to look at the rosters of teams around the country to know that. There's a New York area kid on just about every major college basketball team in the country.

Scouts and coaches are always here, at our high schools, in the playgrounds, at the summer leagues. When the schools from out of town come in, their pitch is to get them out of the city. "What do you want to stay in that rat-infested place for?" We use the opposite approach. "Stay home where your family can see you play, where you will have a great opportunity, where you will get to play in Madison Square Garden ten to twelve times a year." That's why it all depends on the kid, whether he wants to stay home or go away to school.

Travel used to be important when you recruited a kid. It isn't any more because most of these kids are traveling when they're in high school.

What do I look for in a kid? Talent is first. There's no substitute for talent. After that, I'm interested in his attitude. Is he coachable? Will he get along with the other players on the team? Is he selfish or unselfish? I want to know what his work habits are. I want to know about his character, his family background, what kind of kid he is.

So you see, there's so much you have to learn about a kid when you're recruiting him and that's why I like to stick with local kids. We know them. We know their high school coaches.

Recruiting is more competitive, more sophisticated, and more pressing today than it has ever been. And it has become tougher for us because of the Big East. There are always at least ten or fifteen schools chasing the good kids. They come in with t-shirts that have the kids' names on them. They bring video tape of their school, their basketball team, and the community, always painting the best picture, of course.

The Big East has caused us to become more aggressive and more demanding in our recruiting. Certainly, it has made us more competitive and it has changed us a little because we have had to go from a local recruiter to a national recruiter, at least on occasion. That concerns me because we don't know the kids as well and they don't know us that well. I never had great success going out of town to recruit and I never will recruit that much away from our area. Why should I change from the fountain that has brought us everything? It's not as easy to get to know a kid from out of town and you're talking about a $70,000 or $80,000 investment, which is the value of a four-year scholarship.

I once was recruiting a kid and I invited him down here and we took him to the Fresh Meadows Inn for dinner. We sat down and I asked the kid, "Would you like to have a shrimp cocktail?"

"Coach," he said, "I don't drink."

I was happy to hear that, but I wondered how sheltered this kid was. This was some years ago. Today, most kids have been around, they're too sophisticated to say something like that.

I told you my first priority when I recruit a kid is talent. But talent is not enough. As Vince Lombardi said, you have to get people who work hard, people who know how to relate to other people. If a guy won't pass the ball to his mother, if he can't take orders and he won't work, his talent is not enough.

You hear a lot about players not being able to take the pressure. I don't go along with that. One of the things I hate to hear, especially about a kid, is that he choked. Put that same person in that same situation another time, he might come through.

I remember a particular freshman in high school that I coached. We were playing in Madison Square Garden in the finals of the Catholic High Schools championship. We're down by one point and this kid gets fouled with six seconds remaining. This kid goes to the foul line and he was so nervous, the ball got stuck in his hand. He couldn't release it. The referee had to take the ball out of his hand and give it back to him. Now he shoots and the first shot misses by three feet. The second one went into the stands.

It would have been so easy to say he choked, to pass judgment on him from that one incident, and he may never have gotten the opportunity to go to college. That could have destroyed that kid. But he was only a freshman.

In the dressing room after the game, he was crying. I put my arm around him and told him not to worry about it. "You're going to win a lot of ball games for St. Ann's," I told him.

And he did. His name was Willie Hall and he went on to be a great player, a high school all-America who won a lot of ball games for St. Ann's. Later, I brought him to St. John's after I went there and he won a lot of ball games there, too, and became a great player. The moral of that story, I guess, is that you can't judge a kid by one game. You have to see him often, you have to know him, and you have to know what's inside of him. Talent is not the only thing that matters when you recruit.

ELEVEN

Great Coaches and Officials

Through the years college basketball has had some great coaches, legendary names like Adolph Rupp, Phog Allen, Hank Iba, Pete Newell, Ray Meyer, Phil Woolpert, Ken Loeffler, Dudey Moore, Harry Litwack, Jack Ramsay, Al McGuire, and John Wooden. In the New York area, people like Clair Bee and Nat Holman and of course my four mentors, Buck Freeman, Joe Lapchick, Frank McGuire, and Red Sarachek. But never in the history of college basketball have there been so many great young coaches as there are around today; true students of the game who are innovative, creative, dedicated, and very tough to beat. They make it tough on an old guy, but they certainly keep you on your toes.

John Wooden set a standard at UCLA that is truly remarkable when he won ten national championships in twelve years. I don't think that record will ever be approached, much less broken.

There are several reasons why Wooden's record is probably safe for all time. One is that it's much more difficult to win a national title these days because of the field being expanded to sixty-four teams. You have to play more games under such excruciating pressure.

Another reason is the talent is more evenly distributed.

Recruiting and scouting are so much more sophisticated, and there are so many more impact players, no college is going to practically corner the market on talent like UCLA did under Wooden.

For a third, there are more great coaches than ever before who make it tougher to win. They have ways to beat you; they know how to lay traps for you. They also have technical aids, video tape, computers, and a staff that rivals in number the Queen's Guard at Buckingham Palace. In the old days, you only had to concern yourself with beating one coach. Today you have to beat an entire regiment.

Look at the number of outstanding coaches we have in college basketball today. They're scattered all over the map. I'm talking about Lute Olson at Arizona, Larry Brown formerly at Kansas, now with the San Antonio Spurs, Bobby Knight at Indiana, Jimmy Valvano at North Carolina State, Jerry Tarkanian at Nevada Las Vegas, Dean Smith at North Carolina, Mike Krzyzewski at Duke, Bobby Crimmins at Georgia Tech, Gary Williams at Ohio State, John Chaney at Temple, Rollie Massimino at Villanova, Jim Boeheim at Syracuse, and John Thompson at Georgetown. And I have only scratched the surface.

I'm going to give you a rundown of some of the coaches I'm most familiar with from playing against them, how I evaluate them and what I think of their ability. Don't look for any knocks here. That's not my style. If I don't think a coach is good, instead of knocking him, I prefer just not to say anything about him. Besides, I might have to play against these guys and I don't want to give them any added incentive to beat me.

Bobby Knight: We'll start with him because he is probably the most well known coach in our game. Certainly, he's the most controversial. He's the general. If I had to fight a battle, I'd want Bobby on my side. As a coach—a tactician and a motivator—he's first rate. Bobby's a nonconformist. He sticks to what he thinks and what he says right down the line. There are no deviations. This is the way it is and this is how it's going to be. Sometimes he can be a little stubborn, but he refuses to compromise.

As far as his court behavior, I find that difficult to discuss. I'm sure there have been times, upon reflection, that Bobby wished he wouldn't have behaved as he did. Throwing chairs, berating officials. But I can understand that sort of behavior, and I can even relate to it somewhat.

I can remember running around the court myself, knocking down chairs. But I didn't throw chairs at anybody. Mainly, I kicked them. I can remember exploding with obscenities—not at officials, just in general because I was upset. I can remember losing my composure. I think it's all in the way you do it, when and how. I'm sure, on second thought, there are many times Bobby did something he regretted. That's easy to say, but when you're in the frying pan, what can you do? You just explode.

Bobby Knight is an excellent coach. I think he will go down as one of the greatest coaches ever. I hope his temper and his tantrums don't detract from that because his record proves his greatness. He has won three NCAA championships, an NIT championship and an Olympics gold medal and in this post-Wooden era, that's accomplishing something.

Dean Smith: I think my friend Dean-o is one of the most innovative coaches we've ever had. I have to go back to Clair Bee, who was the guru of coaches, so far ahead of his time it was unbelievable. Bee was the first coach I can remember coming up with the idea of multiple defenses. There may have been others before him, but I don't remember seeing them. I remember LIU playing Kansas State at the old Madison Square Garden. Jack Gardner was the

Kansas State coach. LIU was getting the crap beat out of them. All of a sudden, Bee came out for the second half and started changing defenses. Kansas State couldn't figure out what was going on. They were so confused, the next thing you knew, LIU had wiped out that lead and won the game.

Bee was one of the first to do that, long before it became a common practice. He had such a great imagination. Now, I put Dean Smith in that category with his huddle and his run-and-jump and his four corners offense and using his shock troops, running ten and eleven guys in and out of the game. They may have done that years ago, I don't know. My memory isn't that good. But Dean-o does it today and I consider him the most innovative coach around.

Sure he gets great players. He's had Michael Jordan and he came right into our backyard and took Kenny Smith. To win you have to have great players. But there are coaches who get great players and don't win. Dean wins with his great players; he doesn't mess it up. And that has to be to his credit. As far as getting the great players, that's not just luck. Dean is a master recruiter. That's part of his success, part of what makes him a great coach. I don't take points away from a guy for recruiting; I add points.

John Thompson: John was influenced a great deal by Dean Smith and by his career with the Boston Celtics. He believes in the fast break and the pressure defense, both a carryover from his Celtics days. It follows that Thompson also was influenced by Red Auerbach. The Celtics would pressure full court on defense when they had K. C. Jones, which is really the key. You have to have the personnel to play that style of defense.

Like his buddy, Dean Smith, Thompson is an excellent recruiter who gets great players. But he gets them to play. He got Patrick Ewing to play when a lot of people thought

Patrick was lazy or that he just had things so easy in high school, he got by with less than 100 percent effort. John got Patrick to put out all the way and having the ability to motivate your players is part of being a successful coach.

I like what John does. He's another guy, like Knight, who doesn't deviate in a plan, although he can be flexible in his style. He has shown he can play changing defenses. At different times, he has played a box-and-one, a triangle-and-two. He's gone to a 1-3-1 zone or a 2-3.

Thompson's style is difficult to play against and to prepare for because for forty minutes, his teams will hound you on defense. You can't take them prisoners. If they don't get you on offense, they get you on defense. Very often, his defense is his offense. You have to have the players to play that kind of all-out pressure defense, and John usually manages to get the players. But in the end, he knows what to do with them when he gets them.

Rollie Massimino: You have to admire Rollie because he's a self-made student of the game. He never was a great player and he worked his way up from high school coaching, paying his dues. His teams are always among the best prepared and best coached in the country, even though he may not get the quality of players some other colleges get. His crowning achievement was the national championship game against Georgetown. Talk about preparation. Rollie had his team well prepared. He had a plan to beat Georgetown and he got his kids to execute that plan to perfection.

I probably talk on the telephone with Rollie more than with any other coach. I enjoy talking to him, I enjoy being around him, and I especially enjoy beating him. And I know the feeling is mutual.

Rick Pitino: I thought he was on his way to becoming an outstanding college coach when he left Providence College to take over as coach of the New York Knickerbockers. He'll have to stand the test of time, but he's on his way. He got the Knicks into the playoffs in his first season, and they had not made the playoffs in the previous four years before Rick got there.

He didn't make the mistake I made when he took the Knicks job. He had spent a couple of years in the NBA as an assistant, so he understood the pro athlete. And he spent time as a college coach, which has to help him as a tactician. I'm going to sit down with him one of these days and ask him to show me his press. I want to get it down. Sure, why not? I still listen to younger coaches. You're never too old to learn something in this game. If someone had a cure for a disease, wouldn't you try to find out what that cure was?

Jerry Tarkanian: A great coach. Excellent. He was a great zone coach at Long Beach State. He won with that. He was a great coach in junior college. He won there, too. Now, with better players, he's still winning. He's a great defensive coach. He's not given the credit he deserves because of his antics—sucking on a towel, coming up with funny lines— but believe me, the coaches who have to play against his teams appreciate his coaching ability.

Jimmy Valvano: Another coach who may get overlooked because he's such a funny guy, a lot of people don't take him seriously. Hey, there's nothing wrong with having guys like Tarkanian and Valvano in our profession. They're characters, they're colorful, they're good for the game. Jimmy V. gets a lot of attention as a comedian, but he should get just as much as a coach. He's very sound. He's thinking all the time. The job he did in winning the national championship a few years ago when nobody gave him a chance speaks for itself.

On a personal level, I'm very proud of Jimmy's success.

I've known him since he was a baby. Remember, the first game I ever coached, at St. Ann's, was against St. Nicholas of Tolentine, coached by Jimmy's late dad, Rocco.

Then there's Mike Krzyzewski, who was influenced by Bobby Knight when he was Bobby's assistant at Army, but who has stepped out on his own and made his own contribution. Joey Meyer at DePaul, who has a tough job trying to follow his famous father. Eddie Sutton, right out of the Hank Iba mold. And Lute Olson of Arizona. I got my 1-1-3 from him.

Butch Van Breda Kolff, who goes back a long time, is a good sound coach, nothing fancy. He believes in movement of his men and the ball. He plays typical eastern style basketball, which is the result of the years he played for the Knicks. He's probably most well known for having been Bill Bradley's coach at Princeton. He has had a lot of jobs at a lot of schools, but the tipoff on Butch is that he has been successful wherever he has been.

One guy who doesn't get much attention because he coaches in the Ivy League and they can't get the great players as a rule, is Pete Carril of Princeton. Playing against him is like taking a high calonic. He slows the game down so much, you never see the ball. He's a pain to play against. Thank God for the 45-second clock, or you're liable to see scores like 12–10, 8–7 and 3–2 in Pete's games.

I have told you about my defensive guru, Ben Carnevale, who was influenced by Hank Iba, and there was Harry Litwack, a great zone coach, and Jack Ramsay, a defensive genius. I was especially fortunate to be around New York and to watch and play against coaches like Kenny Norton at Manhattan, Don Kennedy at St. Peter's, Jimmy Mc Dermott at Iona, and Danny Lynch at St. Francis, Richie Regan at Seton Hall and Lou Rossini at NYU and Columbia, who would drive you crazy with their box-and-one and triangle-and-two defenses, and my offensive guru, Red Sarachek.

Also Pic Picariello, the longtime assistant to Clair Bee at LIU, who, in my opinion, was the greatest drill master of all time. And P. J. Carlesimo at Seton Hall, who is young and bright and has a chance to be an outstanding coach. I'd better not forget to mention my old St. John's buddy, Al Mc Guire, who was as good a bench coach as you could find and who taught us all a lot about merchandising. Al was the first coach to begin merchandising himself.

I want to make mention here of my assistants, three men who have been with me for years. I consider myself fortunate to have such excellent assistants. Brian Mahoney was an opponent of ours when he played at Manhattan. He was an outstanding college player. He always played well against us. I liked his ability, his intelligence on the court, and his desire. Later, when I was with the Nets, I had him again. In fact, I brought him back to the Nets three times. Guys kept getting hurt and I kept bringing Brian back. He never resented the fact that he didn't play a lot. When I came back to St. John's, I brought Brian along as my assistant.

He left once to coach at Manhattan, but he came back. He's not a St. John's man, which might not have sat well with some people at first. Not now. He earned his masters at St. John's and he's known around the university, by the faculty and by the students. Brian is a hard worker and he's good with people. I give him a lot of authority, just like Joe Lapchick gave me when I was an assistant. He's indispensable to me, great at preparing a team and drilling them. Some day he'll be a head coach again, and he'll be an excellent one. Hopefully, at St. John's.

Ron Rutledge is a young man I recruited. He was a good player and an intelligent player. He's excellent with people and he does a lot of our recruiting. He has no illusions about Xs and Os, although he does them very well. But his thing is working with people, scouting, recruiting.

He's an extraordinary public relations guy. He has a knack for sizing up people, evaluating them, handling them, relating to them. He's bright and he's sensitive to people's feelings and needs. He wants to be a personnel director. Some day he will, and he'll be a good one.

Al Lo Balbo was a great high school coach at St. Mary's in Elizabeth, New Jersey. We go back a long way, Al and I. He was an assistant coach at West Point under Bobby Knight and a head coach at Fairleigh-Dickinson. I used to run into Al a lot at basketball dinners and clinics, in addition to coaching against him. When his tenure ended at Fairleigh-Dickinson, he was available. I needed a man at the time, so I asked Al to join me at St. John's. He's my defensive specialist and an outstanding one. Most of Al's work is done during practice. He loves basketball, he's a good Xs and Os man and he's had a lot of experience and a lot of success.

No discussion of basketball coaches would be complete without special mention of John Wooden, who set a standard of excellence all of us can look at with admiration and respect and maybe a little envy. His critics say he wasn't that good a coach, that he won because he had great players. I don't agree. I think he was a great coach. Sure, he had great material. You can't win without it. But a lot of coaches have great material and don't win a national championship with it. He got great material and he won with it. He not only got there, he stayed there, which is probably tougher. You can't take what he accomplished away from him. You have to give him credit.

I'd like to talk for a moment about one of my favorite subjects, officials. I know what you're thinking, I'm some guy to be talking about officials. You see me on television, bouncing all around the court, yelling and screaming, looking like I'm going a little berserk, and you figure I'm one of the world's worst official-baiters. Not true. I actually have a great deal of respect for officials. I have a soft spot for them. After all, I began my basketball career as an official down in Puerto Rico.

Sure, I have had my disagreements with them. I let them know when I think they have blown a call. That's my duty as a coach. I have to protect my players and I have to fight for the rights of my team. But I think officials, in general, do a great job for the sport of basketball. They give it dignity and integrity.

That doesn't mean I can't have my disputes with them and it doesn't mean that all officials are good. Just like coaches, there are good officials and not-so-good officials. The one code I have always tried to abide by where officials are concerned is never to let a disagreement with them become personal or carry over to the next game.

You have never heard me squawk about officials and you never will. I never have criticized them publicly. I don't complain about them in the papers, and I won't complain about them here. But there are a few things I'd like to get off my chest about officials.

What I tell my players about officials is to act as if they're not there, because when you want them they're not going to be there.

We've all heard the expression officials like to use, "No harm, no foul." Well, that's no harm, no foul to them. A guy is getting banged around out there, who's to say it's no harm?

What I appreciate about referees is that if a guy misses a call, he has the guts to admit it. "Lou, I missed it." When a guy tells you that, what are you going to say? He's been honest. He missed it. He made a mistake. I can accept that. Why do they put erasers on pencils?

What I don't appreciate is when they tell you, "Shut

up and sit down." How can you shut up and sit down? You've got referees working out there, you're working against the opponents, you have hostile fans and he wants you to sit down. You can't. You have to get up. Now they're trying to put straps on you, they've got you in a box. It's crazy. It's not a cricket match. This is a game of emotion, a game of enthusiasm. "Shut up and sit down!"

We played a game against DePaul, a big game in the NCAA playoffs on television. An official blew a call at a critical time. Everybody in the world saw it. Should I have told that official to shut up and sit down? That was a call that might have cost St. John's $200,000 or more. It probably prevented us from advancing in the tournament and who knows what might have happened after that. What could I do about it? I had to accept it. And I never said a word about the call after the game.

That's why I'm serious about this. Why shouldn't we be allowed to sue an official for malpractice? If a doctor performs an operation and messes up, he gets sued. As a driver of an automobile, you have insurance and if you hit another car, you get sued. So why shouldn't we sue an official when he misses a call? If I step out of line, I get slapped with a technical and it costs me $75. What about when the official makes a mistake? Why does he have no fault?

Why not use a television replay on close plays? I know television is not foolproof, but if the replay is conclusive and shows the official missed the call, why not correct it? The way it is, it's like saying the operation was a success but the patient died.

One time we were playing in Madison Square Garden against Fordham. Carmine Calzonetti steals the ball and he dribbles down the court and is going in for a layup. As he does, he passes right in front of me. So I chase him. I go past the Fordham bench, I go underneath and I'm on the court. The referee says to me, "You can't have six guys on the court."

"Why not," I say. "I've been going against seven all night."

Officials are always getting on me for moving on the sidelines. Why do I move around so much? Would you strap a lion tamer? I move around because people are throwing things from the stands and I want to be a moving target. There are other reasons.

One night, we're playing in the Fordham gym against Manhattan College and I'm running up and down the sidelines. In Fordham, the benches are very close together and there's not much room between them to move around. So, I'm in front of Jack Powers, the Manhattan coach, all night long. Finally, Jack can't take it any longer and he complains to the referee.

"Get him out of here," Jack says.

Now the official tells me, "Lou, you can't be there."

"What do you mean I can't be here?" I say. "I can't help it if they have a short runway."

Joe Lapchick used to have a thing that he would do early in the game. There would be a call that would go against us, nothing major and nothing serious. But Joe would slam the chair next to him to get the official's attention. Or he would walk down to the water cooler and just stare down the official. It wasn't that he was trying to intimidate the officials, he just wanted to let them know he was there. That's important for a coach. You have to let the officials know you're there.

Before you get the idea that I'm really ranking on officials, let me say that things are so much better now than they were in the old days, when teams used to be able to pick their own officials. And their methods and their techniques are more consistent. With so many intersectional games nowadays and television serving as a matchmaker, today officials will work both places. And the real good officials never like to be branded with the reputation that they're "homers," that they favor the home team. That's a label the good officials want to avoid.

That's why when I was with the Nets, I used to like it when we got Earl Strom on the road. I wanted him on the road. He was fantastic. He never wanted to be called a "homer."

That reminds me of another story, which really doesn't have anything to do with officials, but shows that coaches can have some fun, too.

We're playing at Seton Hall, coached at the time by that noted television star, Billy Raftery, and we're hot. We're blowing them out of the gym. The second half opens up and again we go on a tear when all of a sudden the Seton Hall manager comes up to me and hands me a note from Raftery. I open it up and it says, "Lou, I surrender. P.S. If you want to practice against a zone, I'll set it up for you. Have mercy. The Raf."

TWELVE

The NCAA

I have had my differences with the NCAA, but by and large I think it does a wonderful job as the governing body of intercollegiate athletics. I also am optimistic about the future because of progressive new leadership headed by Dick Schultz. He is a man who has been in the trenches, having been a coach, an athletic director and having served as chairman of the NCAA basketball committee. I believe he is the right person to lead us into the 1990s. He knows the problems, and more important, he knows the solutions to the problems. I am enthusiastic about his administration.

But that will not prevent me from disagreeing with the association when I think I'm right, just as I have done in the past. One of my disagreements with the NCAA occurred in the so-called Marco Baldi case.

Marco Baldi is a young man who came to us from Italy by way of Long Island Lutheran High School, where we saw him, recruited him, and invited him to come to St. John's on scholarship. There was no problem with any of that. How he got to Lutheran was the problem.

In Italy, there is no such thing as a high school or university scholarship. Everything is done on a club basis,

141

with the Italian National Basketball Federation the governing body of the entire program.

Baldi came from a little town near Milan called Aosta. He was a big kid and somebody spotted him, told the Italian Milan club about him, and they arranged for him to go to Milan to study and play basketball. The way it works, the club has many members and they pay for his education and his board while he is being groomed to play basketball for them. That's all very legal according to their rules, which are under the auspices of the International Olympic Committee.

To help him develop, the Italian team thought it would be a good idea for Marco to come to the United States, where he would play against better competition and improve his game for their benefit. He went first to California, then came to our area. That's how he got to Long Island Lutheran. The Milan club paid his tuition, his transportation, even his room and board. They even brought him back home during the summer so he could play in their league. Again, all quite legal under their system.

Don't we do that here? Don't we give scholarships? Don't we send kids to prep schools?

But the NCAA came in and said nothing doing, that's not legal. The only people who can give scholarships are the schools themselves. No outside agency can give a scholarship. That's in violation of NCAA rules. And that ruling is binding on someone for life.

It didn't matter that all this happened before Baldi arrived at St. John's. It didn't matter that he's not the first European to come to the United States to play after having had his education paid by his club team. It didn't matter that he had done everything in accordance with the rules of his country. No. That's a no-no, said the NCAA. What he did was illegal by NCAA rules. Marco Baldi was being judged by American rules although all this happened in Europe.

There was nothing said until Baldi was almost finished with his freshman season. Then, the day before the start of the NCAA tournament, the NCAA stepped in and declared him ineligible. Great timing, right? I think what happened is that somebody wrote the NCAA a letter about his background. I don't know who, but that's probably what happened. It wasn't that we were trying to get away with anything. We were up front, we had done everything within the rules as we knew them, and we never tried to hide anything. We volunteered all the information as we knew it because we had done nothing wrong and neither had Marco.

But the NCAA ruled Baldi ineligible and he was suspended and prohibited from playing, pending an appeal. We wound up winning our appeal, and Marco was reinstated with the provision that his parents reimburse the Italian club team $11,000 it had spent to send the kid to Lutheran and to fly him back and forth from Italy. Baldi was ruled eligible to play his sophomore year, but as far as we were concerned, the damage was already done. We lost him at a critical time, for the NCAA tournament. I'm not saying Marco Baldi would have led us to the national championship, but he was our big man at 6-11, a workmanlike player who was very important to us and he might have helped us win a couple of games and advance in the tournament.

Baldi was reinstated and he played his sophomore and junior years, but we never got back the games he lost and neither did he, not to mention the embarrassment, humiliation, and bad publicity that resulted for both Marco and St. John's University. All of it for no reason.

As it turned out, Baldi was forced to do something that

was against the rules of his country. He did nothing wrong, but he was the unwitting victim of the NCAA's red tape and archaic rules.

Then there was the Walter Berry case. Walter came to us from high school, but when he came to St. John's, he didn't have sufficient high school credits to graduate. We knew that. Walter came to us as a nongraduated student. He also came to us with the highest recommendation of a neighborhood friend and adviser. He went to the wall for this kid. The friend practically pleaded with us to take him. He praised Walter's work ethic, his desire, his intelligence. He said this was a kid who was not afraid to work hard and wanted to make something of himself. He said we wouldn't be disappointed if we took him, and that person was right.

There is a program at St. Johns—and at some other universities—designed specifically for just such students. It's called the GED Program and it requires taking remedial courses. It stipulates that a student, who is a nongraduate from high school but who comes with the proper recommendations, may be accepted. The student must take twenty-four credits in his first year, regular college courses, no special courses and no eligibility for athletes. If he passes those twenty-four credits, he is then accepted as a full-time student and, in the case of an athlete, he is eligible to play in his second year.

Walter enrolled in that program and did everything the rules stipulate. In fact, he did more than was necessary. He volunteered for extra work and actually took thirty-six hours, but he was credited with only twenty-four hours.

This is not a program that was made for athletes. We had it at St. John's for fourteen years and Berry was the first athlete ever to take it, but it was something that was familiar to the NCAA. Others had done it at other schools and were eligible to play.

The problem with Walter Berry was in the terminology. In our catalogue, it states that such a student is nonmatriculated. That's when the NCAA stepped in and said they would accept the program only for matriculated students. The National Education Society in Washington said Berry qualified. New York State said he qualified. But the NCAA said he didn't and ruled him ineligible for his second year, all because of a technicality and the language. The program was acceptable, it was the terminology that wasn't.

Rather than sit out a second straight season, Walter left and went to junior college. I couldn't blame him.

That's what I mean about the NCAA being too bogged down with rules with no provision for relaxing those rules. Somewhere, common sense has to come into play. And intent has to be taken into account. In both the Baldi and Berry cases, everything was above board. There was no intention to cheat on anyone's part, the university, the athletes, or the outside agencies involved. It was just a matter of interpretation of the rules that affected both players. The NCAA should not be so unbending. It should take into account the intentions of all parties. But first and foremost, it should always have the best interests of the student-athletes at heart.

Hopefully, that will all come about under Dick Schultz. Already, from what I have heard and what I have seen, he has relaxed some of those rules. I don't mean relaxed them to the point where people are taking advantage and getting away with something, but relaxing them to where common sense, intent, and the best interest of the athlete are considered.

The NCAA is going to have to take a good, hard look at its rules. Half of its rules are outdated and don't make sense, even if they were put in there to catch the cheaters. Our Lord gave us Ten Commandments and look at all the problems we have. When I started coaching, the book was an inch thick. Now it's six inches thick and things have not gotten any better. You need a law degree just to understand the thing.

Can we give a kid a cup of coffee? A Coke? No, you can't do it. There has to be some common sense involved in the rules. Intent has to be considered. But I can't get mad at the NCAA. Why? Because we're the NCAA, the schools themselves. We make up the NCAA. So I can't get mad at the governing body, although I feel its judgment has been very narrow. There are always going to be cheaters. There are always going to be people trying to bend the rules. There are going to be some schools looking to take home the chandeliers. It's up to the NCAA to differentiate between the cheaters and those who make an honest mistake because of their interpretation of the rules. And, I repeat, that's where common sense comes in.

How about this rule? Only the head coach and two assistants can go to a high school game. My third assistant coach cannot see a high school basketball game, even as a spectator. What if he has a son playing high school basketball? What if he wants to see his nephew or his neighbor's kid? What if he just wants to be involved in his community and watch his local high school team play? Nope. Can't go. The NCAA forbids it because if he goes to watch a high school game, for whatever reason, theoretically he's evaluating and that's against the rules. See, common sense again.

We were invited to the White House once. Another time, Governor Mario Cuomo invited the team up to visit the Governor's mansion in Albany. Both times, the NCAA turned us down, which I can't understand.

Here's another rule. If you take a kid into school and he doesn't score 700 on the college boards, under the regulations in Proposition 48, he has to sit out a year. He can't practice. He can't do anything until he gets his grade point average up to 2.0 for 24 credits over one academic year. The concept is good, but we should allow him to practice. By not allowing him to practice, we're hurting him in two ways—he's not eligible to play for a year and he can't even keep his skills sharp. It's like exiling him to Elba. To me, that's not good common sense. Even prisoners in Sing Sing get an hour of recreation every day.

I just think the whole thing is unfair. Not only do you stop a kid from playing, but you disassociate him from the team for a year. What is the purpose of this? To punish him? Or to make him a better student? Why take that year away? Is the purpose to make him study harder in high school? I don't know. And we're punishing a kid not once, but twice. Why can't he go to school for five or six years? The ordinary student can go to school for four and a half or five years and nobody says anything about it.

Let him practice with the team two times a week under the supervision of a dean. Let him feel like he's part of the team. The idea is to improve his academics, not take away his athletics. Why give him an athletic scholarship in the first place? Because he's an athlete. He's not an academic genius. If he were, we'd give him an academic scholarship.

The NCAA is going to have to take a hard look at whether we should pay our athletes. I think we should. I said that facetiously many years ago, but now it's a serious consideration.

Many grievances have to be taken care of. We have too many rules for too many schools. The rules have to be changed in the NCAA and maybe one of the solutions to our problems is to pay our athletes. Think about it. If you're playing in the upper echelon, like some football teams that are drawing 90,000, 100,000, 110,000 fans to every game, allowances may have to be made.

I don't think the answer is that you give a kid $10,000 because if you do, somebody's going to give him $20,000 under the table. You can't stop that. But there could be some acceptable form of compensation for athletes.

What would be so wrong about having a special league made up of those big athletic powers, the schools that make a lot of money off their athletic programs? Put them in a special category and work out some form of compensation for those players who are accepted in those schools because of their athletic ability.

Let's face it, we're professionals and our athletes, for all intents and purposes, are treated as professionals and they have neither the experience nor the maturity to handle it. We're making stars out of them at eighteen and nineteen years old. We're putting so much pressure on them.

When we first had pregame meals, these guys would eat the table. Now, they sit down, take a bite and walk away. They can't eat; they're too nervous. And we did it to them.

I'm not saying paying them is the answer to our problems. It won't eliminate the cheating. But some adjustments have to be made by the NCAA. Why can't we give our athletes some sort of monthly allotment to take care of their bare necessities? Maybe like they do at the service academies. A kid who's playing intercollegiate athletics can't go out and work. There simply isn't time if he's going to practice, go to class, and have time to study. Working is out. My kids start at nine in the morning and they don't leave until eight at night. That's a long day.

What kind of wages do we pay them? They get their tuition, books, room and board and fees. But if they had a job, they could earn a lot more money and they wouldn't have to put in such long hours. They're doing all this for the exposure and the opportunity.

So, why not just subsidize them? We're professionals, aren't we? We charge admissions, don't we? And the pressure is all on the kids.

I think our kids are going to organize. There's going to be a union of college athletes, you'll see. It's coming. How are we going to prevent it? Let's not put our heads in the sand. There's going to an organization of college athletes, a body to which athletes can take their grievances. Some kid is going to look at that arena, see 60,000 paying customers in there and say, hey, what am I getting out of this? Why am I working so hard? For what, books, tuition, and fees?

The players are the pawns. Are we using them? What do they get out of this? Education. Exposure. A chance to play in the pros. That's fine, but there are some scars, whether we like to recognize them or not. Everybody says how great it is for the kids to have this opportunity, but is it really that great for them?

What if they're not good enough to make the pros? What if they don't get their degree? Then what do they have to show for all their hard work? That's what we have to be aware of and concerned with. Not the superstar. He's going to be all right. We have to be concerned with the ordinary player.

I know the arguments on the other side. I've even used them myself. We're giving them the opportunity to be exposed to college for those who might not otherwise get the chance. Half an education is better than no education. What they do with that opportunity is their responsibility, we say. But is it? In the final analysis, it's the school's responsibility. It always comes back to the school and the coach.

Let's say a kid goes to school for four years and at the end of those four years, he has thirty credits. Whose fault is that? The school has to bear at least some of the responsibility. I'm not saying everybody has to be Phi Beta Kappa, but he has to at least get close to a degree after four years or have the opportunity to graduate in five or six years. Here at St. John's, we have had many of our athletes come back and take the credits they need for their degree after they had gone on to try their hand at pro ball. George Johnson is one who comes to mind. He came back to school and got his degree. We try to encourage that and many of our kids take advantage of that opportunity, which is to their credit.

That's one of the reasons I refuse to stand in a kid's way if he wants to leave school and turn pro before he has used up his eligibility. We have used this kid for two, three years, and he has very little to show for it in return. So, if he wants to leave school and earn some money, cash in on what he has done, we have no right to stop him. I think they should become professionals if they're ready. The majority are not going to be ready, but some are and they have the right to capitalize on their success. It's as if you were a great artist or a great musician and somebody wanted to take you out of school to make a living off your talent. Nobody has the right to stop you from doing it. We can't just look at intercollegiate athletics as the minor leagues for professional basketball and football. These kids have rights, too.

As coaches we have a tremendous responsibility to these kids. Maybe too much responsibility. We're responsible for their performances on and off the court; not only for their playing, but for their academics, their dress, their comportment, the company they keep, their manner of speech. We have them two and a half to three hours a day, enough time to exert a great deal of influence.

What about the professor in class? If this is an educational institution, and we, as coaches, are part of it, then we are educators. But have we taken on too much responsibility as coaches? What about the professors? Do they have a responsibility to that individual? Do they take the time to know the problems of the students in their classrooms? Is the student having trouble with his girl friend? With his parents? Is he on drugs? Does he have a drinking problem? Why isn't he performing up to his capabilities? I would hope the professor knows who his student is, that he takes the time to understand the student, ask him things, develop a relationship, instead of just treating the student as a number.

As coaches, all that is expected of us. We're putting ourselves in a precarious position, taking on a tremendous responsibility. A coach has to be a problem solver, a policeman, a psychologist, a father confessor, an educator, a disciplinarian, a role model, an adviser, and a friend. We have to be all things to all people. When I walk into my office in the morning, I never know what's going to hit me, what problems I'm going to have to deal with. Not only do I have to worry about my own problems, I have to worry about the problems of every kid on my squad.

Through the years, I have coached a hijacker, a wife beater, a shakedown artist, one kid who died of an overdose of drugs, and another who was accused of making more than 5,000 obscene phone calls.

Sports is a great teacher. Where in this world can you learn to take orders and not sulk? Where can you learn to take suggestions from your teammates? Where do you learn to take adversity? A bad call by an official, you have to live with that, win or lose. Where do you learn to rely on the help of others and to help them out? Where do you learn to be gracious in victory? More important, where do you learn the ability to bounce off the floor when you lose and come back the next day?

These are the lessons of sports that can be transmitted into life. Some of the greatest students, Phi Beta Kappas, have experienced only success. What happens to them when they go out into the world and experience failure for the first time? They can't recover. That's why the big companies like IBM and Xerox want kids with an athletic background. Because they've been competitive. They have suffered adversity. They know what it is to fail. And they have resiliency; they can bounce back.

That's as much of an education as learning a formula, memorizing a poem, or learning the parts of the body. I understand where they're coming from, but what bothers me sometimes is if you do poorly in class, they suspend you from athletics. If a kid misses a layup or lets a guy walk in on an offensive rebound, we pull him from the game. Why don't they take a kid out of the math class if he messes up? If a kid does poorly in the classroom, he's not allowed to practice. But if a kid does poorly in practice, he's still allowed to go to biology class.

People complain that we, as coaches, make a lot of money. That's only a minority. Think of the thousands and thousands of coaches in high schools and junior colleges, in Division II and Division III and many in Division I who never make any money and the great job they do as educators.

Are some coaches overpaid? Is it right that they earn more than a law professor or a professor in a medical school? A lot of professors think they're being cheated, there's a little jealousy, we get too much publicity, we get paid more than they do, in some cases. The great Adolph Rupp of Kentucky hit it right on the head, I believe. He spoke for all coaches when he told this story.

One Saturday morning, Adolph drives up to the gas station in his big, expensive Cadillac. In comes the math professor, driving a model-T Ford.

"Hey, Adolph," says the math professor. "Here I am a big professor, I have my masters, I have my doctorate, I've been to several universities, and I'm driving a model-T Ford. You're only a basketball coach and you're driving a big, beautiful Cadillac."

And Adolph, in his own inimitable way, says, "Professor, suh, if you had to square the hypotenuse in front of 14,000 people every Saturday night, you would drive a Cadillac, too."

THIRTEEN

Basketball Overseas

I was at my camp in the summer of 1978 when I got a call one day from Ed Smith, a St. John's alumnus working for the State Department.

"Lou," Smith said, "we'd like you to go to Portugal to conduct a basketball clinic for us."

"Portugal," I said. "Who the hell plays basketball in Portugal? They're all five feet, two inches tall."

"It's important," Smith said.

"How important?" I asked.

"Very important," Smith said.

He went on to say that the purpose of my trip was more than just to teach basketball.

"The Communists are getting a foothold with their young people," he said. "We want to get them back on our side and we think basketball is one way we can get the young people to listen to us."

I took the first plane I could get. It was Labor Day. I arrived in Lisbon and I was met at the airport by a man named Bob Douglas, who was the Director of Operations in Portugal for the State Department and who had been a law enforcement officer in Boston. For two days Douglas briefed me.

"What we want to do, Lou," he said, "is give a clinic for coaches. We feel the coaches can influence the kids."

He went on to say that the Communists are ruling by fear. They're trying to take over Portugal and they intended to do that by getting to the kids. If we could get our coaches involved through sports and reach the kids, we could turn the thing around. That's why they wanted me there, and I was only too happy to accept.

While I was in Portugal, I got to make a pilgrimage to one of my favorite shrines, Fatima. As we traveled to Fatima by car, I noticed a busload of kids, all carrying red flags. That hit home because of what Bob Douglas had told me. Douglas also told me that there was 35 percent illiteracy in the country and it was the goal of the United States to educate the young people of the country and get them to understand our way of life.

The United States Ambassador to Portugal in those days was Frank Carlucci, now the Secretary of Defense. It was his job to try to rid the country of Communism, and I was to be one of the instruments in that plan. Secretary Carlucci did a tremendous job for his country and I can only hope I was able to play even a small part in his success.

There was a lot of cloak-and-dagger stuff going on around me. While I was with Douglas, he would take me in one door and out another. One time he pointed to a doorway.

"See that," Douglas said. "That's where the Cuban ambassador was shot."

I spent a week conducting clinics in Porto, Portugal, where they make the world's greatest port wine. They had twenty-seven or twenty-eight coaches attending these clinics and they seemed very eager to learn. They asked questions, offered theories, and we exchanged ideas. It was a very rewarding trip. I was well received, everything went smoothly, and there were no incidents. And I came home with a great appreciation for Portugal—its history, its warmth, its beauty, and its port wine.

I enjoy traveling. I find it very educational. And I certainly have done my share, starting with Uncle Sam sending me on trips when I was in the Coast Guard. The travel has continued throughout my coaching career, especially since the game of basketball has grown worldwide.

I have been all around the world. It's one of the rewards of my profession. I have met popes, ambassadors, and ministers. I have seen voodooism. I have been to the Canary Islands, Angola, Montserrat, Spain, Italy, Portugal, Brazil, Canada, France, Argentina, Yugoslavia, and Greece. You name it, I have been there.

Without question, my most memorable trips have been to Italy and through the years, I have made many friends in my parents' homeland who remain my friends to this day. One of these friends is Cesare Rubini, whom I met in 1966 and who had been Bill Bradley's coach when the senator from New Jersey was studying at Oxford and playing for the Simenthal club in the European Cup League. Rubini told me as far back as 1966 that some day Bradley would be President of the United States. He based his prediction on the fact that when they played the International Cup, they traveled throughout Europe, and wherever they went, Israel, France, Spain, the first thing Bill always did was pay a visit to the United States Ambassador in that country and learn all he could about the country he was visiting.

When I first went to Italy, the ball was a little square. It's round now. They have made tremendous progress.

I was asked by Rubini to conduct a clinic for five or six hundred coaches, a request I gladly accepted. It would turn out to be a most interesting and enjoyable trip, but it started out as if it would be anything but enjoyable.

Mary, Enes, and I landed at Rome Airport and when we arrived, we discovered that our luggage was lost. It turned out that it had been sent to Hong Kong instead, so for three days, until our luggage could catch up with us, we found out who our friends were.

One of our bags did make it through. It was a bag in which I was carrying instructional films that I intended to use during the clinic. We had to go through customs and the agent asked me what I had in the case.

"Films," I said.

"What do you mean films?" he said.

"Just films," I said.

I was ushered into a private room where another customs agent took out a book and he said something about penal code 245. He was going to have to confiscate the films.

"What for?" I said. "There's nothing in there. They're just basketball films, look at them."

They didn't buy it and we had to go see a general who told us that the films had to go out of the country to be checked before we could get them back. I didn't realize it at the time, but they were checking for pornographic films.

Eventually I got my films back and conducted the clinic at the Palazzo Dello Sport, where they played the basketball games in the 1960 Olympics. That was another experience. They wanted to film everything we did, which made the clinic drag on longer than it should have. Not only that, we kept having all kinds of delays.

One day, they forgot to bring film for the cameras. Next, they had trouble with their cameras. By the fourth day, after they had fixed the cameras, the two cameramen assigned to take the films had become so irritable with each other, they started arguing, then beating the crap out of one another. I don't know if they ever got any films of the clinic, but the big thing that came out of this trip was the relationship I formed there, the bond that grew between the members of the Italian Basketball Federation and me. We have maintained that friendship through the years. I have been back to Italy many times, by myself and with my team, and they, in turn, have been our guests at St. John's on many occasions.

The highlight of my trip to Italy was when we were taken to Castel Gandolfo, the summer home of the Holy Father. We walk into this large hall and there must have been 10,000 people there, groups from all over the world.

They introduce the group from Ireland and the place goes wild, screaming and yelling. Madison Square Garden at its wildest couldn't compare with the noise they were making.

Then they introduced a group from Africa, another from France, another from Spain. All of a sudden, the door opens and in comes the Holy Father, Pope Paul VI, being carried on his chair. It's pandemonium. People are yelling and screaming and singing.

A little priest from New York is standing next to me. He sees the Holy Father enter the hall and tears start streaming down his face. He has just seen his boss and he couldn't control his emotion.

It's easy to get caught up in the emotion when the Pope makes his appearance. People were grabbing at him, at his clothes, trying to touch him. People are crying, they're cheering, they're yelling, they're singing. It was unbelievable.

The Pope spoke in five different languages. Then he called for the Italian delegation, of which we were part, and the next thing I knew we were being ushered up to the Holy Father and we're standing right in front of him. He knew we were Americans, so he spoke to us in English. I was so flustered and nervous, I answered him in Italian. He probably said to himself, "This guy speaks Italian," so he spoke to me in Italian. And I answered in English. Now it's getting to be a regular Marx Brothers routine.

It must have been obvious to him that we were nervous because he began to smile. Then my daughter Enes took over and she was able to converse with the Holy Father in Italian. They were supposed to take pictures of us with the Holy Father, but the guy who came along to take the picture forgot to get film for his camera. The official Vatican photographer took some pictures, so fortunately we got them. I have a copy on my office wall of the picture of Mary, Enes, and me standing with the Holy Father.

The whole thing was very moving. I have heard about people facing the Holy Father and just becoming speechless. I can believe it because it's so emotional.

I would have loved to have met Pope John XXIII, but I never had the opportunity. I was going to present him with a St. John's basketball shirt, extra large, with the number 23. Knowing the kind of man he was, I think he would have appreciated that.

As I have said, my trips abroad were most rewarding because of the bond of friendship that I formed with so many people, among them Pedro Ferrandiz, the coach of Real Madrid. He is one of the great basketball coaches in the world, having won four or five European titles.

Ferrandiz came to the United States once to sign a kid named Whitmore from Notre Dame to play for his team in Spain. Whitmore's agent was Arthur Morse and Ferrandiz had a meeting with Morse to work out the details. When Ferrandiz told me he was coming to the United States, I invited him to spend some time with me at St. John's.

One day he said to me, "Lou, do you know where I can get $10,000 in a hurry?"

He needed it, Ferrandiz said, to give to Arthur Morse as a deposit to close the deal for Whitmore. I told him, "I'll lend you the money," and I withdrew the $10,000 from the bank and gave Ferrandiz the check. I never even asked him to sign a paper as a receipt, which I admit was not very smart of me. I was taking a big chance. He could have gone back to Spain and I'd never see him again and I'd be out

$10,000. Worse, God forbid he could have had a serious accident, then how was I to prove he owed me $10,000?

When I told Mary what I had done, she went wild.

"Are you crazy?" she said. "You didn't even get anything in writing?"

This was 1968 and $10,000 was about all I had to my name. I didn't know Ferrandiz very well. I had been in his company only three or four times, so I really was taking a big chance. He could have flown the coop with my money, but I had a feeling about him. And I was right. A week later, a check for $10,000 arrived from Spain, and that was the start of a great relationship that still exists to this day.

One time I went to the Canary Islands to represent the United States in the formation of the World Basketball Federation. Dean Smith and Joe B. Hall came with me as U.S. representatives and there were coaches from all over the world, twelve hundred coaches from fifty-four nations. One of our goals was to get the Chinese delegation involved. Why? Because there are six million coaches in China. Imagine that. Not six million athletes, six million coaches. We figured it would be a feather in our cap to have six million Chinese coaches as members of our Federation.

I'll never forget it. It was a beautiful, sunny day on this marvelous, picturesque island. They brought the Chinese delegation in, a four-man delegation consisting of the head coach, his top assistant, an interpreter, and a political attache. Everybody gets introduced and, through our interpreter, we tell them what we have in mind—an international federation of basketball coaches. The Chinese delegation takes one look at the Russian coach, Andre Gomalski, and they say, "If they're in the organization, we're not joining." And they turn around and walk out. That's when I first realized that we're dealing with more than just basketball here.

Another time I was invited to lecture at the First

Spanish-Arabic Clinic in Madrid for five hundred coaches, 135 of them from Arabic states.

I'm giving my clinic. It's a brutally hot day, but I'm really into it. I'm dripping with perspiration, but I'm on a roll. I'm breaking down defenses, going like a house afire, sailing along, the sweat pouring down. I'm really involved. Every coach is wearing a head set so that what I'm saying in English is coming to them in their native tongue through an interpreter. All of a sudden, a hand goes up in the back of the room, so naturally, I figure the guy has a pertinent question about some point I'm making. I stop my lecture and call on him.

"Coach," he says. "When is the next bus to Madrid?"

"What?" I shout. "You blankety-blank. That's why you interrupted my lecture? What am I, the friggin' tour guide?"

Montserrat. Joe Adams, President of American Trucking and a St. John's alumnus, asked me through Father Dirvin, a vice president of St. John's, if I would give a clinic in Montserrat where Adams had a home. I was happy to oblige.

Montserrat is a British island in the Caribbean and they didn't know much about basketball. Soccer is their sport. So four of us went. Father Dirvin and I and two of my players, Glen Williams and Bernard Rencher. They treated us like royalty. They put us up in a big, beautiful house near a golf course. The house had two levels. I was on the top level and on the lower level was the kitchen and Father Dirvin's bedroom. It was a beautiful location, a typical Caribbean scene.

One night, we went out to dinner and we met some people who started talking about voodoo and spirits on the island. It was getting very involved and they were getting into it very deeply. But I'm skeptical. I figured they were just trying to lay some local color on us. But Glen Williams, who is originally from St. Thomas, says, "No, Coach, they really believe in this stuff."

Now we go back to the house and go to sleep and all of a sudden I wake up from a deep sleep and I have this funny feeling, a premonition. "Somebody's after Father."

I open my eyes and from the light of the moon I can see a shadowy figure. I knew right away it couldn't be Glen or Bernard because the guy wasn't big enough. I flick on the light and all I can see are these two green, piercing eyes staring at me. I yell at the guy and start chasing him as he turns around and takes off.

"Father, Father," I'm yelling. I wake up the whole house. Now Glen is chasing the guy, but he had a head start and Glen couldn't catch him, even with his long strides. Glen did find Father's wallet, which was empty. Apparently, the guy had gotten into Father's room, taken his wallet with $100 in it, then he came to my room and took my passport. We figured that when I saw him, he was on his way back to get the gold chalice that Father was going to use to say mass in the morning.

The next day, we appeared before the constable to report the theft. I described the guy as best I could and the constable said he knew who he was because it's a small island, only 10,000 residents, and they know everybody. Apparently, this guy had a record. I don't know if they ever caught him, but Father was out $100 and I had to have a duplicate passport made.

The funny thing is that it was the second time in my life that I had such a premonition. The other time was the night my father died. I had gone to his house because he was very sick and we knew he didn't have much time left. The family was keeping a vigil around the clock. It was getting late, so Mary and I went home. I fell asleep, but all of a sudden I woke up out of a deep sleep.

"Pop is dead," I said to Mary. Sure enough, five minutes later, I got a telephone call telling me Pop had died.

Another memorable trip was the one I made to Angola with an all-star team made up of players from the Big East. Carmine Calzonetti of St. John's, one of my former players, told me, "Lou, they want you to go to Angola for a clinic."

Angola was a Portuguese territory that has been war-torn for more than a decade. When I got there, I felt I was back in World War II seeing Yokohama or Tokyo. There was so much poverty and rubble in the land. Our visit was obviously something special because six hours before we arrived, the bombing stopped, and six hours after we left, it started again.

We gave clinics to local coaches and played games in an arena that was packed with 15,000 spectators. It was the first time "The Star-Spangled Banner" had ever been played in the country. Our kids did a marvelous job at the clinics. They represented their country very well and they were very well received. The kids loved us. I had met Antonio Cuneo on my (earlier) trip to Portugal, and now it turns out he is the coach of the Angola team.

One day, they had a picnic for us on an island and we saw a lot of poverty, people living on the shore, living in huts. There was an old man fishing on the shore, dressed only in a cloth that was wrapped around his body. Our players saw this and were so moved by it, they took off their sweaters and shirts and started handing them out to the people. It made me feel so proud of those guys seeing them give of themselves like that.

We traveled everywhere by bus. One day, as we were on our way to the arena, the bus passed a young girl. She couldn't have been more than sixteen or seventeen. She had a big basket on her head. She had a baby by the hand, another on her back and she was carrying a third. You couldn't help feel for her. She was hardly more than a child herself.

Some of our guys had a hard time adjusting to the lifestyle. They got sick. They couldn't drink the water and the food was terrible. But they survived and did the best they could. It was an interesting experience to say the least.

One day, they took us into the bush for an excursion. We started out by bus and we traveled an hour and a half to two hours, driving, driving, driving, through the country, a lot of barren land, wild beasts all around us. A typical African scene. Now we get to a bridge and they stop us. There were Cuban soldiers there and two or three trucks, Russian-made trucks. They're talking back and forth and we're getting a little worried, wondering what all the talking was about.

My assistant coach, Ronnie Rutledge, and I were getting a little uneasy. After all, we were responsible for these kids. Finally, they tell us to get off the bus and they put us onto these Russian trucks, manned by Cuban soldiers. There were 20,000 Cuban soldiers in the country at the time. They put us on the trucks and we go through the jungle, until we come to a clearing. And on the top of a hill is a stockade.

"Oh, oh," I thought. "Here we go. They're going to kidnap us. We're gone. They're going to do away with us. All these stars from the Big East are going to be wiped out."

We go up the hill very slowly to a stockade and they stop us again. There are soldiers up there. And they start another conversation, which gives us that uneasy feeling again. All of a sudden, the trucks turn around and we go back down the hill and into the bush again. Then the trucks get stuck and everybody has to get out and push. We were scared and it was an uncomfortable situation, but it turned out they were merely taking us for a ride to show us the countryside.

The food was lousy and the conditions were horrible

and we had some uneasy moments, but it turned out to be an interesting experience, although I wouldn't want to do it too often. We were treated as well as could be expected given the poverty in the country and the warlike conditions that prevailed.

I had a previous commitment, so I had to leave early. The day before I left, some guy who said he was from North Carolina came to me and handed me a letter.

"Do me a favor," he said. "When you get back to the States, mail this letter for me."

I asked him why and he said he didn't want it to get intercepted. He was working for a rubber company, and I suspect he was CIA. That's the atmosphere that existed there, mystery and terrible conditions.

I hated leaving the kids there, but everything worked out fine. They returned home safely, having had a tremendous experience and the satisfaction of having done something for their country.

Of course, basketball is not the main thing with most of these trips. The real purpose is to try to cement relations with these people and sports is merely the instrument the State Department uses. As I travel around the world, even to Communist territories, I find that basketball is growing. The people of the world know our teams and our players. They know St. John's and other college and pro teams from video tapes and from the "Game of the Week."

I'm not saying that basketball is going to cure the ills of the world, that it's going to bring people together. But it certainly helps. I'm proud of our kids for doing their part and I'm grateful for the opportunity to do my part.

FOURTEEN

Chris Mullin

Early in the 1987–1988 season, in our sixth game, we went to Los Angeles for a game against UCLA that turned out to be a nice trip. It was the second week of December and it was good to get away from the cold of the East. We won the game, which always makes for a nice trip, and to make it even better, we won on national television, ABC carrying it as its "Game of the Week" in college basketball.

As it turned out, the Golden State Warriors were playing the Los Angeles Lakers the next day and I got a chance to talk to Chris Mullin. He called me at our hotel just to say hello and wish us luck. He said he wanted to try to get to our game, but his schedule didn't permit it.

It was good to hear from "Mo." He sounded happy and excited about the way things were going for him in the NBA. I think it did him a lot of good to talk to somebody from home. I had the feeling that even though he was now in his third season with the Warriors, he was still suffering from a case of homesickness. He was 3,000 miles away from home, from his family and friends, and even though he was doing well in the NBA, he is a New York kid and very close to his family. Mo had a little trouble adjusting to being away from home.

167

We had a nice talk and when it came time to say our goodbyes, he wished us luck for the season, and I wished him luck and I promised Mo I would try to get over to Madison Square Garden when the Warriors played the Knicks. I wished him well and told him to keep up the good work, that all of us at St. John's were proud of him.

Mullin always will be special to me. He was such a good kid and such a great player, and he led us to some of our greatest successes. There's no doubt that he will go down as one of the greatest players ever to play at St. John's, the first basketball player from our school to make the United States Olympic team. Here's a kid they said couldn't run and couldn't jump.

When he was in grammar school, people said forget about it, why don't you play baseball? You're too slow and you can't jump. He's a sophomore in high school and they said forget about it. He's too slow and he can't jump. Now he's a senior in high school and a hundred guys are looking for his services. Nah, don't go to a big school. You're too slow. You can't run and you can't jump. He's now a freshman right here at St. John's. He's named first team all-Big East. Again, the people. He's too slow, he can't run and he can't jump. He's a sophomore and he gets invited to the Pan American team. Then he gets invited to the Olympic team. He's Co-Player of the Year in the Big East with Patrick Ewing of Georgetown and an all-America. Again the doubters. Yeah, he's OK, but he can't run and he can't jump. He wins the John Wooden Award as the outstanding player in college basketball. He gets drafted in the first round. Again, he'll be all right, but he's too slow. He can't run and he can't jump. He just signed a contract for $2 million. Can you imagine if he could run and he could jump?

I had known Mullin since he was a little fellow. I got to know the whole family and I became fairly close to them. I watched Chris develop as a player in high school, recruited him, and watched him grow as a man and a basketball player after he came to St. John's.

I have never known a more dedicated kid than Mo. He was hardly ever without a basketball in his hands. He even did something that I had never had any player do. He asked for a key to the gym and many nights he would let himself into the gym, switch on the lights, and begin shooting baskets. It could be ten, eleven o'clock at night and if the lights were on in the gym, you'd know it was Chris Mullin in there shooting baskets.

All his hard work paid off. In his senior year, we made it to the Final Four of the NCAA tournament, finishing with a record of 31–4, the best in St. John's history. He was named winner of the John Wooden Award, given to the outstanding player in college basketball, and he was the number one draft pick of the Golden State Warriors, the seventh pick in the country.

At first, Mo had a tough time in the NBA. He went through a contract dispute with the Warriors, then when he reported to camp, he was terribly overweight and out of shape. That was unlike him. It took him most of the season to lose the weight and finally get his game together. But he finished with an average of 14 points a game and began to make a solid contribution to his team by the second half of the season. In his second year, he improved in all phases of the game, raising his average to 15.1 points a game. And early in his third season, he was giving every indication that he was on his way to being the solid, outstanding professional basketball player everybody said he would be.

I was glad to have had the opportunity to talk with him and on the plane ride back to New York, I thought about our talk and I had a good feeling about it. I was also looking forward to seeing him play when he came to New York. I had no inkling of what was to come. Not the slightest clue.

We flew all night from Los Angeles and I got home at about 3 A.M. Mary was waiting up for me and when I came in the door, she told me she had heard on the television earlier that night that Chris Mullin had checked himself into a rehabilitation center because of a problem with alcohol.

"What?" I shouted. I couldn't believe it. I thought it must have been a mistake. I was stunned. It was especially hard to believe after I had just talked with him the day before. He had given no indication that he had such a problem. Why didn't he say something to me if he was thinking about checking into a rehab center?

When you hear something like that, something that just comes out of the blue, the first thing you do is begin to think back, to see if you could make some sense of it. It was like somebody had told me my own son was an alcoholic. How could it be? How could I not have known, not have seen some signs?

I remembered seeing Mo earlier in the season when the Warriors came to Madison Square Garden to play the Knicks. He had scored about 17 or 18 points that night and he looked great. He was happy to be home, around his family and friends, and he had played well for them and that made him feel good. Then I remembered seeing him all summer at my camp. He came up to help out and to get in shape for the season. He ran three to five miles every day. He got himself into great shape. He looked good and he felt good. I saw no indication that he was drinking too much.

Then I had talked to him in Los Angeles and, again, there was no indication that he was having a problem. He sounded good and he seemed happy. That's why this was all so hard to believe.

I knew Chris liked to drink beer, but I never saw any indication that it was a problem, apparently because he handled it. That's something I can see now that I couldn't see before. His performance? Never a problem. Rumors? Of course there were rumors. But you're always going to hear rumors, especially about a star. If he scores 20 points instead of 27, there are going to be rumors. A star can't have a bad day without the rumors starting. We're all going to have bad days. As a coach, I have bad days. But a star can't have a bad day because then the rumors will start.

He was like any college kid as far as I could tell. I knew he drank. I thought it was an occasional beer or two, no more and no less than any kid his age. But a problem? I had no idea.

He drank with his family. What's wrong with that? Didn't I, as a kid, have a glass of wine with dinner with my father's approval and supervision? I swear to you, I never saw him drunk, never saw him tipsy. There's a story that he was drunk on the plane on our way home from Denver after we made the Final Four, but I never saw it. He was celebrating. It was the greatest victory we ever had, so Chris had a few beers, but I wasn't aware of any commotion or any problem.

Later, I heard that somebody saw him and knew he had had too much to drink. This guy was sitting in the first class section and Mo was in coach and they had run out of beer in coach, so the guy in first class gave him a beer. Why did he give it to him? And why didn't the guy tell me if he thought Chris had had too much to drink?

I love my wine. A glass of vino with dinner. But is it a problem? No. So how can I tell a kid not to drink? How can I deny him what I do myself, especially if it doesn't seem like a problem? That's part of growing up, too, learning how to handle it. How come colleges sell beer on campus?

We made trips to Europe and Africa and you couldn't drink the water, so I told the kids they could have a glass of beer, wine, or a soda with their pregame meal. Many of them took beer and I don't think there's anything wrong with that. I drank wine. There never was a problem. None of the kids ever took advantage of it.

In the old days, before the legal drinking age was raised to 21, the kids were allowed to have a glass of beer with dinner at our annual sports banquet. Again, nobody abused it, maybe because we were right there. But how can I control what they do when I'm not around? Look, all these years, forty years in the game, and how many guys have I had who had a problem? Two? Three? And in those cases, I found out years later that they had a problem.

I never thought there was anything wrong with a kid having a beer after a game. I had seen Chris have a beer, but I never thought he was overdoing it or that there was a potential problem. Believe me, if I had, I would have done something about it.

Perhaps that sounds naive, considering all the time I spent with him. But he never abused his drinking in my company and there never were any warning signs that he had a problem. He couldn't have performed as well as he did if he had a drinking problem.

Maybe the problem escalated after he left St. John's, and I don't mean to pass the buck. But I knew Chris was lonely and homesick and that might have contributed to his drinking. In fact, it did come out later that he spent many nights alone in his apartment, drinking beer.

The loneliness, the pressure. He has been under pressure constantly from the time he was in high school. Then college, the Olympic team, All America, College Player of the Year, number one draft pick, the contract dispute. That kind of constant pressure builds up on you.

I love the kid like he was my own. Such a good kid. The day before he was going to leave for the final Olympic Trials, I had to give a talk out on Long Island. I'm coming home and it's 10:30 at night and I said, "Damn, I've got to call Mo. Got to wish him good luck," because I could see he was a little uptight about the trials. I said, "I bet the sonofagun is in the gym." So I drive by the gym and the lights are on and sure enough, who's in the gym but Mo and his brother and they're shooting baskets.

I hugged him and wished him luck, but you could see the pressure on him was tremendous.

This is a kid who was away every summer. All over the world. The Orient, South America, Europe. This is a kid who could never say no to anybody. He's such a good-natured person. You can ask him to do anything, he'd do it. People ask him to do a thousand things, he'll do them all. Or try to do them. You can't do everything, but he'd try because he's that kind of person. He always has time for little people. He was never too important for anybody, no matter how successful he became.

When he was with me, the kid never missed a practice, never missed a game. He had tendinitis once and we stopped him from playing for three weeks. His father came in one day and said, "Coach, you have to do something. Chris is getting up early every morning and running three to five miles." He wanted to play so bad, we had to threaten to put a cast on his foot. That's the kind of kid he is, that's how dedicated to basketball he is.

After he was in rehab a couple of weeks, he called me. It was good to hear his voice.

"Coach," he said, "I'm doing fine. I'll be OK."

Soon after he got out of the clinic, he was in New York for the All-Star break and I asked him if he wanted to be a guest on my television show. I told him I would understand if he preferred not to do it, but he came through like a trouper.

"No, Coach," he said. "I'll do it. I want to talk about my problem. It's good for me. That's part of my therapy."

I was glad he did the show and I think he was, too. I was so proud of him, the way he handled himself. It made me feel that the rehab really helped him a great deal. Whatever they did for him, it helped.

Three times he said, "I'm an alcoholic." I just listened to him and I said to myself, "If it can happen to this kid, it can happen to anybody." You can't say he came from a family where there wasn't love. You can't say there weren't people around for him when he needed them.

He said something that really shook me up.

"Coach," he said, "I have the same thing as a person who has a predisposition to diabetes or cancer. I can't have a drink for the rest of my life. Not even one for St. Patty's Day. I've got to go one day at a time, one hour at a time."

He was saying things I had never heard from him before.

"Coach," he said, "I was trying to be too perfect and you can't go for perfection. You have to go for progression."

I sat there in awe, listening to him and I was so proud of what I was hearing, so proud of how he was reacting. I couldn't help thinking that I wish I had been able to detect his problem when he was with me, that I wish he had come to me. If he had, it would have been between him and me and his family. I would have addressed the problem, but it would have been confidentially.

If a kid ever comes to me, that's what I would do, keep it confidential. I don't think I have the right to make it public because if you come to me for help and you come in good faith, man-to-man, it's like going to your doctor or your psychiatrist or your attorney or your confessor. It's nobody's business. If I don't keep that confidentiality, then how can I ever ask another kid to come to me with a problem, no matter what that problem is?

I looked at this kid who once had the whole world at his feet and I realized he's got an illness. He can't have a drink for the rest of his life. He's got a tough road ahead of him and he's out there in the world, he's vulnerable. There are people who are going to want a piece of him as long as he's a star, and he's out there alone, and if he falls, he's going to have to pick himself up and start all over again.

I love this kid and I pray for him to make it. And I know he'll make it because he wants to make it. You could tell that by the way he played after he came back from rehab. Played better than ever because he was working harder than ever. He's such a good kid and he's been successful all through his life. He always was a hard worker and now he has to work harder than ever before, but he'll make it. I know he will.

FIFTEEN

Gambling and Drugs

If I was so shocked to hear about Chris Mullin's addiction to alcohol, one reason is that through the years I have tried to be so diligent about two other insidious problems that have attacked intercollegiate athletics that I was caught completely off guard about alcoholism. I'm talking about gambling and drugs, two evils that have ruined the careers, and the lives, of a countless number of great athletes. I guess you can say it was a case of me guarding the door while the enemy was coming in through the window.

Drugs is this generation's sickness, the most serious threat to the very fabric of athletics, both professional and intercollegiate. In the early part of my career, it was gambling—more specifically, point-shaving—that almost destroyed intercollegiate athletics.

Basketball is the sport most vulnerable to point-shaving for many reasons. There are only five men playing on each side at any one time and any one of them can affect the outcome of a game. It's probably the easiest sport in which to hold back or slip up without arousing suspicion. And, most important, a player who is involved in a fix need not cause his team to lose a game, merely not win by as many points as the "line" the oddsmakers have put on the game.

I have lived through four point-shaving scandals, so I have a pretty good idea how it works, how easy it is to fix games and what destruction it can cause. I have seen great players, all-Americas, have their careers and their lives destroyed. I have seen some of these players go to jail, and others banned from the NBA for their involvement. For a couple of hundred quick dollars, they threw away careers that would have brought them hundreds of thousands of dollars.

This is one of my major concerns as a coach. I worry about it day and night, and I take every precaution to do what I can to prevent it from happening again. And let's not be naive and put our heads in the sand. It can happen again if we're not careful. Kids today are just as vulnerable as they were twenty and thirty years ago, even though the financial rewards are infinitely greater for a professional basketball player than they used to be.

If we take the attitude that it can't happen again, or that it can't happen to us, that's the first step in making certain it does happen again. You have to be on your guard constantly, every season, every game.

Actually, there have been four point-shaving scandals in college basketball, but the first one occurred in the 1940s. I was just a kid and I knew nothing about it. But the next three hit home and had a great impact on me.

The second scandal was in the fifties and it rocked the world of college basketball to its foundation. Big names were implicated. That one had a profound impact on me because I was in college at the time and deeply involved in the game of basketball and the mapping of my own coaching career.

The third and fourth scandals really hit home. They came in the sixties and seventies and I was well into my coaching career at the time. They shook me, mainly because I thought we had progressed to the point that it wouldn't happen again. I believed the lessons of the first two scandals would be deterrents to any more. They weren't. If it could happen a third and fourth time after it had happened twice before, I say it can happen again and that's why I say we have to be aware that it can happen again and we have to be on our guard.

Look at the pattern. Each of these scandals came about ten years apart. There was one in each of the last four decades. If that pattern continues, that would mean another scandal in the eighties. Thank God, it hasn't happened yet, but that does not mean it couldn't still happen in this decade, or the next.

I hope not, but we cannot afford to lower our guard.

What can we as coaches do to prevent it? I can tell you only what I have done, and continue to do.

First, I think we have to understand that our kids, our athletes, are nothing more than a cross section of society. They come from all parts of the country, from all ethnic and economic backgrounds, from big cities and small towns, from thriving metropoli and from rural areas. Whenever you get that kind of a mix, in those great numbers, you are going to have cheaters in all fields; you are going to have people who will look to cut corners, people who will look to make an easy dollar.

What is our obligation?

Number one is to inform and educate them of the dangers that are there. And to let them know about the consequences. We can't sugar-coat it. We have to let them know the stark reality. If you get caught shaving points, you can go to jail. You can lose your career. You can lose your life. You can lose your family. Hey, it's happened. Kids went to jail. There were jails back then. There are still jails.

The first day in school, when the team assembles for the first time, that's one of the things I tell them. I give them dates and incidents. I name names. I give them facts, from actual cases. We have a scrapbook at St. John's with newspaper clippings from previous scandals. Who did it. What they did. How and when they were caught. What their punishment was.

Next, I have my players read the rules book. It's from Public Law 88-316, the 38th Cong. S. 741, 6 June, 1984. This is what it says:

To amend title 18, United States Code, to prohibit schemes in interstate or foreign commerce to influence by bribery sporting contests, and for other purposes.

Be it enacted by the Senate and House of Representatives of the United States of America in Congress assembled, that (a) chapter 11, United States Code (entitled "Bribery and Graft") is amended by adding at the end thereof the following new section:

<u>   </u>SPORTING CONTESTS, BRIBERY
18 USC 201-218

224 . . . Bribery in sporting contests
　　(a)　　Whoever carries into effect, attempts to carry into effect, or conspires with any other person to carry into effect any scheme in commerce to influence, in any way, by bribery any sporting contest, with knowledge that the purpose of such scheme is to influence by bribery that contest, shall be fined not more than $10,000, or imprisoned not more than five years, or both.

<u>78 STAT. 203</u>
<u>78 STAT. 204</u>

　　(c)　　As used in this section
　　　　(1)　The term "Scheme in commerce" means any scheme, effectuated in whole or in part through the use in interstate or foreign commerce of any facility for transportation or communication;

(2) The term "sporting contest" means any contest in any sport, between individual contestants or teams of contestants (without regard to the amateur or professional status of the contestants therein), the occurrence of which is publicly announced before its occurrence;

(3) The term "person" means any individual and any partnership, corporation, association, or other entity.

Signature ＿＿＿＿＿＿＿＿

When that has been read, we hand out to each player another form that reads as follows:

ATHLETE'S PROMISE

I (the undersigned) hereby solemnly promise to report to my coach and the moderator of athletics any attempted bribe, whether I consider it serious or a joke, or for failure to report such event, to abide by the decision of the President of St. John's University to dismiss me dishonorably and immediately from the university.

Date ＿＿＿＿＿＿ ＿＿＿＿＿＿＿＿＿＿

＿＿＿＿＿＿＿＿＿＿
Coach

＿＿＿＿＿＿＿＿＿＿
Moderator of Athletics

After they have read the rule and the statement, we discuss it. We take it sentence by sentence so there is no mistake. Do you know what this is? Do you understand it?

Are there any questions? Any doubts? Do you understand that you are obliged to let us know if anybody approaches you about fixing a game or shaving points, even if it sounds like a joke? You have to report it to us. We have had players come to us and say, "Coach, there's this guy who's been bothering me." I tell them, if he does it again, let me know and I inform the authorities immediately. It might be nothing, but I can't take that chance. Our thing is we don't want the kids to decide if it's a joke or not. That's our job. But even we don't decide, we let the people who are experts in such matters decide if it is serious or not.

Once the players have read all this and we have discussed it and I am convinced they understand it, then they sign it.

We don't let it go at that. We talk about it all the time, constantly reinforcing the dangers involved and the consequences. In November, we bring in authorities from local law enforcement, people familiar with gambling. We bring in Edward A. McDonald, the Attorney-in-Charge of the Organized Crime Strike Force for the United States Department of Justice, and his aide, Mario Sessa. They come with their task force and these people talk to the kids about the scandals of the past, what to watch for, what the consequences are. We bring in judges from the Supreme Court of Kings County. They come in and let them know if they're caught, this is what can happen. They can go to jail. Repetition. Constant reinforcement. We can't emphasize it enough.

When the season starts, we keep reinforcing it. When we go on the road, we have a rule: No telephone calls are put through to the players' rooms. All calls must go through the coach. Even if it's an emergency. And we try to keep all the players together after 4 P.M. That makes it more difficult for anybody to get to them because it's harder to get to a player when he's in a group than it is when he's alone.

But I'm not fooling myself. Even with all the precautions, if a guy wants to cheat, he's going to cheat. If he wants to do it, he'll find a way.

Usually, it's going to start out in a casual way. Nobody's going to come up to a kid and say, "Hey, do you want to dump a game?" It will never happen like that. And it's not going to be a stranger. It's going to be somebody who's going to try to befriend the player first. He's going to do that over a period of time, either directly or through a friend. He's going to infiltrate, try to gain the player's confidence. He's going to slowly try to get that kid in a situation where he can gain control of him.

He might take the kid out to dinner, buy him a gift, spend money on him, treat him like he's special. He might introduce him to a girl. The goal is to put the kid in a situation where he is hooked and he can't back out.

We have to tell our kids these things if they have never been exposed to them. They don't know about it. There's no doubt in my mind there are people out there who are trying to hook into kids in high school, to begin the progression that can lead to another scandal. We have to let our kids know that a situation can start if they're not ready for it, so we try to get them ready for it, to be on their guard against somebody trying to get their hooks into them. We try to emphasize to a kid that he can be set up with a dinner, or the introduction to a girl.

Here's a hypothetical case, which actually has some basis in fact. A friend will come up to a kid after a game and say, "Congratulations, you played a great game. You won that game by 30 points. Here's $100, take your girlfriend out to dinner and a show on me."

Innocent enough, right?

Well, next time, the same guy will go up to the kid and say, "Hey, good game. You won by 30 points, but why don't you just win by 10? There's $500 in it for you if you do." And, just like that, boom. Gotcha.

Especially if the kid is predisposed. If he needs the money or thinks he won't be detected. A kid in college today is smart enough to know that's wrong. In the earlier scandals, most of the kids they got to were going to do it anyway because they got caught up in a situation. There are always people who are going to take short cuts; people who can't see beyond the $500 they're going to put in their pockets and the things that $500 can buy.

That kid is going to be tempted and he's going to get caught. Maybe he needs the money. Maybe he got some girl in trouble. Maybe his family has a financial problem. There are so many things that could get a kid to do that and these parasites who feed off these kids are going to find out their weakness.

The kids of today get more information about the dangers of point-shaving. At least I know they do at St. John's. I don't know what happens at the schools where the coaches have never been through this. I'm not making any accusations or being holier than thou, but I have been through this three times. We know what can happen. We were brought up with that thing.

A lot of people say it can't happen again because of the potential earnings of a kid who becomes a professional. But there have been players who threw that all away in the past. And what about the kid who knows he's not good enough to play in the NBA, but is a starter and is good enough to influence the point spread? That kid has an opportunity to make money here and now.

It's there and for us to deny it is crazy. And don't tell me it's only in New York, only in the big cities. If you're going to do business, do it in a small town. In New York, everybody talks.

Another thing, it's not only players who are vulnerable. How about coaches? And referees? Nobody is exempt.

The history of the scandals is that first it was the money,

then it was girls, then it was drugs. A progression. Whatever it takes to hook a player, they'll use it, and drugs is the most logical way these days. That's the sickness of today's society. Again, it's not just athletes. It's all of society.

The drug thing is nothing new, although it's more widespread today. In the 50s, I had a player who had been Mr. Biddy Basketball. A good-looking kid, the all-America boy type. He played for me in 1954. Two years later, he was dead of a drug overdose.

Thank God I have never had a drug problem at St. John's. I've had my suspicions about some players, but I've never had a problem. I'm not foolish enough to think it can't happen.

What would I do if I found out a kid was using drugs? You have to catch him first because you can't go making accusations without proof. If I catch him, or he comes forward and admits his problem, I'm not going to report him to the authorities and have him put in jail. If I know a guy has a problem, the first thing I'm going to do is tell his parents. Then get him to a doctor, into treatment. My job is not law enforcement. I'm going to get him immediate help.

There are signs I have been taught to look for. Like irregularities in his behavior that are totally different from the person you know. Maybe he's starting to get sloppy in personal habits or on the basketball court. He becomes careless. He's not dependable. You're not going to see it in his performance, at least not right off. That usually comes in the late stages of drug addiction and, when I get the kids, they're young; you're probably not going to see his performance suffer too much unless he started using drugs when he was eight years old.

The best way I can explain it is this: how does a doctor know when something is wrong with you by looking at your tissue? Anything that is not normal is abnormal. And that applies here. When you look at a person's personality, you know what his normal behavior is. If he deviates from that behavior, a light goes on. The first thing you do is talk to the kid. You have to do that. You owe him that.

You bring him in, sit him down and talk to him. "There are rumors," you tell him. "Do you have a problem? Tell me. That's what I'm here for. I'm here to help you."

Some of them will lie to you. Some just don't care. They feel they can handle it. These are all the things a coach has to look for. He has to know his kids as if they were his own. It's no different than being a parent. In some ways, you're closer to them than their parents. You spend more time with them.

We bring in people from the outside to talk to them. People whose business it is to deal with this problem. People in law enforcement. People who run rehabilitation clinics. The team doctors, Dr. Ralph Squitieri and Dr. Irwin Glick. You try to educate them, inform them as much as possible about the dangers of drugs. What the addict goes through. We have movies, lectures. We do all that. Is it enough? No. If a guy wants to do it, he's going to do it.

My function as a coach is to inform them, to let them know it's out there, you have to be on your toes. And you hope you have saved one kid or prevented one kid who might be weak from turning to drugs. If you do, then all the hours put into this are worthwhile.

It's a very difficult situation for a coach. You may get to them before they've tried anything. And you may prevent one kid from trying it. They're not going to come out and say, "Hey, here I am." It's something a coach today has to be attuned to, just like a father has to be attuned. We're like parents because it's in society and it's a cross section of society. It's the well-to-do and the people who are not of means. There's no pattern and no exemptions. It's all around us.

I tell my players: you can't blame your environment. You can't blame your parents. That's a cop out. And you can't say you didn't know the dangers. It's all around you. On television, in the newspapers. As a coach, you preach, you preach, you preach, but in the final analysis, it's the individual who has to say no. Like the slogan, "Just Say No."

Do you worry about it? Of course you do. Coaching has changed so much. There are so many more problems. Even the automobile is a problem and it never used to be. In the old days, kids didn't have cars. They couldn't afford them. They took public transportation to school. Or they lived on campus. Today, every kid has a car, or his family has two cars and he drives one. And they'll have a few drinks, then get behind the wheel of a car.

I talk to my players over and over about these problems, drugs and gambling. I remind them constantly. Watch your company. You go to a party, there's no doubt in my mind there's going to be stuff passed around at some of these parties. You have to walk out. It's like drinking. If you have a beer, everybody thinks you're a drunk. The other guy can get falling down drunk, nobody cares. But you're in the limelight. You're different. You're like Caesar's wife. You have to watch everything you do.

So, as a coach, you talk and you talk, you preach and you preach, you warn and you warn, you remind and you remind. You do this constantly, over and over. But in the end, it really comes down to the individual you're dealing with. And I'm convinced you have to have a lot of luck going for you, too.

SIXTEEN

Willis Reed

A little past the midpoint of the 1987–1988 National Basketball Association season, the New Jersey Nets called a press conference to announce they had hired Willis Reed as their new head coach. They signed him to a contract for the remainder of that season and two more seasons. I couldn't have been happier if I had a son and he was hired to coach the Nets.

I suppose I always will have a soft spot in my heart for the Nets, which you might say is one of my alma maters, even though it has been years since I worked for them. But as far removed from the team as I was, I always have been interested in who their coach was. I suppose it's natural to take an interest in the line of succession that follows you in any job. I was overjoyed that Willis Reed was now in a job I once held. I consider Willis one of the finest people I have ever met in the game of basketball and one of my closest friends in the game.

I'm not sure exactly when and how our relationship started. It just sort of grew out of casual and frequent contact. We seemed to be thrown together quite often, either through mutual friends or our mutual love for the game of basketball. We would appear at banquets together or at clinics and camps and the friendship just seemed to blossom.

Other than basketball, there wasn't any common denominator between us. In fact, you could search for years, go to every part of the country, and you probably couldn't find two people who are more unlike each other, all the way down to our physical stature. Willis is a strapping and imposing six feet, ten inches tall, which is more than a foot taller than I am. He's black, I'm white. He's from the country, I'm a city boy through and through. He was a great basketball player, a Hall of Famer, I was a bench warmer. There's even a big difference in our ages. I'm about twenty years older than Willis, which puts us in different generations, I guess.

But despite the differences in our ages and our backgrounds, I never felt a generation gap between us and I never felt we had any trouble relating to one another.

I can remember the first time I ever saw Willis Reed. It was the first time he had ever been in New York. He was a senior at Grambling College, the star of its basketball team. His game was completely physical at the time. He was big and strong and tough, but terribly unpolished. Still, you could see the enormous potential he possessed and the tremendous desire he had.

The 1964 Olympic Trials were held at St. John's, so I had an opportunity to watch the games. That was one of the greatest aggregations of basketball talent ever assembled in one place. It included Rick Barry, Cazzie Russell, Bill Bradley, Wally Jones, Lucious Jackson, Jim (Bad News) Barnes, Mel Counts and Larry Brown, who was playing with an AAU team at the time. And Willis Reed, who more than held his own against those bigger name stars, most of whom came from bigger schools and had national reputations.

Willis wasn't selected to the Olympic team, although I thought he deserved it. But the competition was so tough and he didn't have the reputation of some of the other big men, like Counts, Barnes, and Jackson. As it turned out, it may have been a blessing in disguise. He was drafted by the Knicks and he didn't have to miss training camp. A lot of those guys who went to the Olympics were late reporting to camp, but Willis was there from Day One and that might have helped him make the transition from college ball to the pros.

I didn't get to meet him during the Trials, but since he was in New York, our paths crossed from time to time. The Knicks practiced at St. John's and I frequently went to Madison Square Garden to see them play. Little by little, I began spending more time with Reed, getting to know him a little better.

At first, he was very shy and a little backward because of his country upbringing. He seemed a little lost and bewildered in the big city. Through the years, I watched him grow into a sophisticated and urbane New Yorker, a growth in his personal life that was mirrored as a basketball player. He not only became the captain, but also the heart and soul of those great Knicks championship teams in the early seventies. I never saw a more fierce competitor on the basketball court than Willis Reed.

As his career flourished and he became more sophisticated and more in demand for appearances, I had the opportunity to spend more and more time with him. He had a basketball camp in upstate New York and so did I and we would visit one another's camp to conduct clinics. The more I got to spend time with Willis, the more the friendship grew and the more the friendship grew, the more I came to admire and respect the man.

He even helped me try to recruit Julius Erving out of high school. He found out that we were interested in having Dr. J come to St. John's and Willis volunteered to call Erving and talk to him about us. I didn't ask him to do it, he suggested it. Needless to say, I appreciated his help and I never forgot it. As it turned out, Erving went to the University of Massachusetts instead, but not because of Willis. In fact, one of the reasons we even had a shot at Julius was because Reed talked to him about our program and about the advantages of playing in New York City and in the Garden.

Reed's career ended with the 1973–1974 season. Three seasons later, he was named to succeed Red Holzman as the team's coach. With no previous coaching experience, he managed to win forty-three games, more than the Knicks had won in four years, and get them into the NBA playoffs for the first time in three years. I thought he did an excellent coaching job, especially for a guy with no coaching experience. Given a few years under his belt, I thought he had a chance to be an outstanding coach.

The Knicks never gave him the chance. Fourteen games into his second season, Reed was replaced as coach. As it turned out, the Knicks would have to wait three years before they won as many games as Willis did and before they made the playoffs again, testimony, I think, to the job Willis did for them.

He never said so, but I know Willis was hurt by what the Knicks did. He thought he deserved better, that he had earned a longer shot. But he never complained, either publicly or to me in private. That's not his style.

One day he said to me, "Lou, I'd like to come over and spend some time with you and just observe." I said I would be happy to have him and the next thing I knew, he was coming every day. He'd attend practice and he'd come to our games. He was spending so much time with us, working with the kids, we decided to make him an assistant coach. But we had our full complement of coaches according to NCAA rules, so the only way Reed could join us would be trips. It was on one of these trips that I had one of my most frightening, and one of my most comical, experiences. That is, it was frightening at the time, but it's comical now that I can look back at it.

I was at my basketball camp in Sidney, New York, and I arranged a hunting trip for Pop, Willis, and me. This is another thing that has always endeared me to Willis—the way he got along with Pop, treated him with respect. Pop, don't forget, was twice Willis' age, yet they were buddies. Pop liked Willis very much and I think Willis felt the same way about Pop.

It was early autumn and we were bird hunting. It got to be about three o'clock in the afternoon and we decided to break up and go separate ways to flush out the birds before it got dark. The plan was for the first one who spotted a flock of birds to blow his whistle or call out to the other two. So Pop took off in one direction, Willis in another direction, and I in a third direction. My plan was to follow a wall that I was told would bend around and end up right in front of the house where we were staying.

OK. I take off. I start walking and I'm walking and walking and walking and the wall is not bending; it's staying straight. Now, it starts getting darker. I call out, but nobody answers. So I keep walking and it keeps getting darker and darker and I'm getting lost. I don't hear any voices. I don't hear any shots being fired. I didn't come across any people. Nothing.

Now it's pitch black. All the trees look the same to me. I had no idea where I was. I'm screaming. I'm blowing my whistle. Nothing. I keep walking and I start yelling, "I'm lost. God Almighty, I'm lost." Still nothing.

In my mind's eye, I can picture the headline in the next day's newspapers.

"CARNESECCA LOST"

"P.S. He's Been Lost for Years"

as a volunteer. I told him if he wanted to do that, he woul
be welcome, but we couldn't pay him.

He was more than willing to accept. He said he wasn
interested in the money, what he wanted was to get th
most out of it that he could, to learn as much as he could
He worked as hard as any assistant coach worked. He neve
got a dime because it was against NCAA rules. In fact, i
cost him money. We couldn't even pay his travel expenses
but he made every road game and paid for it all himself. I
felt bad, but Willis understood and, again, he never complained. He was doing it because he wanted to. He never
missed a game, home or away. He never missed a practice.
And he helped us. He did a good job with our big kids.

Naturally, the kids loved having him around, not only
because he was such a great player, but because he's such
a great person. He was terrific at motivating kids to play
hard all the time, which is the way he played.

I knew he wanted to get back into coaching and this
is the kind of guy Willis is. He didn't brood and he never
indulged in self-pity. He never talked about what a bad
break he got from the Knicks. He didn't think he could just
sit back and wait for people to offer him another job because of who he is. He did something about it. He worked
hard at improving himself, at learning more about coaching. If another job came along, he wanted to be as prepared
as he could be. You have to respect that in a man.

One day he said to me, "Lou, one day I'm going to
coach again. I'm going to show them I can coach." And I
always believed that.

It was while he was working with me as an assistant
that Willis and I became really close friends. I found out
that we shared a few other interests in addition to basketball. He liked pasta and red wine like I do. And he loved
hunting and fishing. So we wound up going on hunting

Now I start to panic. I'm thinking I'm going to have to spend the night in the woods and I'll probably freeze to death. Suddenly I remembered something Pop once said. Follow the stream. It will take you to a bridge. And usually, if there's a bridge and a stream, there will be a road nearby. Sure enough, I follow the stream and I see a house on top of a hill. The lights are on in the house. Thank God, I'm safe.

I trudge up to the house, tired and out of breath, and I knock on the door. I'm holding my hunting rifle in front of me. A lady comes to the door with her little girl. She opens the door and sees me standing there with my rifle and she screams and throws her arms in the air.

"No, no," I said. "Don't be afraid, lady. This is not a stick up. I was hunting and I got lost. Can you help me? I'm from Golden Valley."

After I calmed her down, explained who I was, where I came from, and what had happened, she agreed to drive me home. When I got to the house, tired and hungry and upset, I had to hear it from Pop.

"Where you been?" he yelled. "We calla the state troopers."

I told him I got lost.

"How you canna get lost?" he said.

He really gave it to me. He wouldn't let up all night. I felt like I was a little kid again being chewed out for being late for dinner. Later, I found out that I had been given the wrong information. There was no wall that curved and came to the house. I had no idea where I wound up.

"Luigi," Pop said. "You'd geta lost coming back from Holy Communion. Here, nexa time you usea this."

And he handed me a compass.

Willis and I still talk about the incident and every time I think about Pop, I think about that night and it puts a smile on my face.

Soon after he coached with us, Willis got his opportunity. Creighton University hired him as its head basketball coach. He did a good job there, had some good teams, but it wasn't a good situation and he left. There was an opening for an assistant coach with the Atlanta Hawks. Mike Fratello, the Hawks' head coach, called me and asked about Willis Reed.

"Grab him," I suggested to Mike. "The guy's good. He'll help you."

Willis got that job, then when Bill Russell took over as coach of the Sacramento Kings, Willis went with him as an assistant with an understanding he would move up to become head coach when Russell went back into the front office. Before that happened, the Nets offered Willis their coaching job and he took it. It was the right choice. He had no idea how long it would be before Russell gave up coaching. Besides, he would be more at home back in the New York area, where he had his greatest success, where the press knew him and liked him, and where he had so many friends.

That's why I was delighted when he took the job with the Nets. I still believe he'll be an outstanding coach when he gets the right players. He works too hard to fail.

The amazing thing about Willis Reed, as I look back at the years I've known him, is how much he grew and matured from the country kid he was when I first met him. One thing Willis once told me really impressed me and has stayed with me.

"Lou," he said, "don't let anybody handle your money. Pay for the best advice, but you handle your own money." I took his advice and got myself an agent and I'm glad I did. And I pass that advice along to my kids.

Even after he left, I stayed in touch with Willis. I would call him from time to time, or he would call me. The man is one of the greatest people on God's earth. He does not have a malicious bone in his body.

Now that he's back in the New York area, I'm hoping we can get together more often. I might even go hunting with him during the off season. This time, I'll remember to take my compass.

SEVENTEEN

The Players

In my coaching career, I have had relationships with hundreds of players. I don't know the exact number, but if you figure forty years of coaching, fifteen players each year, accounting for those who played more than one year, that probably comes close to four hundred players who have played for me either as a head coach or assistant in high school, college, or the pros.

I have had great players and some not-so-great players, over achievers and some who never lived up to their potential, hard workers and some who looked to take the short cut to success. But I'm proud of all of them and I stay in touch with many of them, some who go all the way back with me to my first high school team.

I've said it before and I'll say it again: the players have always come first with me. The players win, not the coach. For that reason, you'll never see me criticize one of my players in the press. I can't do it. I never will. Where would I be without them? I'd be slicing salami in a deli somewhere.

I believe you can never criticize players because that would destroy their confidence. My job is to build confidence, not destroy it. Even if you have a team that you know is not good enough to win, your own pride won't let you think you can't win. And I can never give my players the idea that I think that. That's why, collectively or individually, I will never criticize a player in public. Oh, I'll take a player aside, face-to-face, one-on-one, and criticize him if I think he's not putting out, if he's not working hard enough, not making the most of his ability. But in public? No. You can never destroy their confidence in public.

The one thing I have always asked of any player is that he give me 100 percent, and I mean in practice as well as in games. It's an old saying, and a true one, that you play the way you practice. By that I mean, if you cheat during practice, take a short cut, you are likely to do that during a game.

"Nothing happens in the performance that doesn't happen a thousand times in the rehearsal."

You know who said that? Toscanini. And it's true. It applies to just about everything. If a player goofs off in practice, I won't show him up in public. I just won't play him, that's all.

As a coach, I believe you have to treat players differently, just as you have to treat your children differently as a parent. I'm not talking about two sets of rules or a double standard. What I mean is that some players you have to stroke, others you have to kick in the butt. Some you have to build up, constantly tell them how good they can be; others you have to put a rein on, hold them back. Some you have to be on constantly or they will take advantage; others you know will always give you 100 percent effort. The important thing as a coach is to find what it takes to motivate an individual and work on it.

You can never lose sight of the fact that all players, like all people, have their pride and their ego. You can never take that away from them.

The press and the public, and even the players, get too

caught up, I think, in who starts and who doesn't. I have a saying I like to use:

"It doesn't matter who starts. A lot of people started world wars and lost."

I once heard Red Auerbach say the important thing isn't which five guys start the game, the important thing is which five guys finish the game. And I couldn't agree more.

A lot of people have asked me who my favorite player has been that I have coached. I would never get into something like that because there have been so many and it wouldn't be fair to all the others to single out one, or two or a dozen or fifty. They're all important. Every one of them, down to the guy who was the least successful.

I have been blessed to have been associated with so many great players; two of them were named winner of the John Wooden Award as college basketball's Player of the Year in consecutive years—Chris Mullin and Walter Berry—and another, Mark Jackson, who was Rookie of the Year in the NBA in 1987–1988.

I had great players in high school, like Danny Powers and Larry Tierney, Donnie Lane, Tommy Kearns, Hugh Kirwin, Tommy Hunt, Max Dente, Willie Hall, York Larese, and Donnie Burks.

I was associated with great players when I was Joe Lapchick's assistant. People like Alan Seiden, Gus Alfieri, Lou Roethal, LeRoy Ellis, Kevin Loughery, Ivan Kovac, and Tony Jackson, who was the greatest shooter I've ever seen. I think about TJ playing today with the three-point shot and it boggles my mind to imagine what he might have done.

In the pros, I coached Rick Barry, one of the greatest players ever to play the game.

I've had my share of kids who became outstanding professional players, like Billy Paultz, Johnny Warren, Mel Davis, Reggie Carter, George Johnson, Sonny Dove.

The list is really endless and I hesitate to mention one because it's impossible to mention them all. But a kid like Sonny Dove always was special to me. I was broken up the day I learned he died in an accident. He had such great promise. There were the Cluess Brothers, Kevin and Greg, and the McIntyre Brothers, Ken and Bobby. And Rudy Bogad and Joe DePre, Billy Schaeffer, Tony Prince, Ed Searcy, Mel Utley, Beaver Smith, Glen Williams, Trevor Jackson, Bernard Rencher, Wayne McKoy, David Russell, Kevin Williams, Billy Goodwin, Bob Kelly, Carmine Calzonetti, Ron Rowan, Willie Glass, Frankie Alagia, Jeff Allen, Bill Wennington, Mike Moses, Ronnie Stewart and Shelton Jones.

The greatest tribute to a coach, I believe, the biggest thing is to see a kid reach the limit of his potential, whether it is in basketball or in life. Donnie Burks, for example. I had him in high school and college. He was an outstanding basketball player, but he was a shy kid, I think because he stuttered. He had a hard time dealing with people at first. But he worked hard and he overcame his handicap and wound up being an actor who did many television commercials and had a featured role in the hit Broadway musical, *Hair*. A thing like that really makes you proud to be a coach.

I'm proud of Ronnie Rutledge, who played for me and is now one of my valued assistant coaches. Ronnie wasn't a great player, but he was a hard worker and he has become a fine person who one day will be an outstanding personnel director for somebody.

Another one of my favorites is Mark Jackson, who had such a great rookie year for the New York Knicks. In my opinion, he was the one most important factor in turning the Knicks around and I was thrilled when he was named Rookie of the Year in the NBA, an honor he richly deserved and truly earned.

Why is he a favorite of mine? Not because he became

a great NBA player. Because he worked so hard to make himself great. Because he made the most of his ability.

When the Knicks made him their number one draft pick, there were a lot of people who criticized them for their selection. They said Mark wasn't big enough, he wasn't fast enough, he wasn't a good enough shooter. It just goes to show you that sometimes mistakes can be made.

What they didn't know about Mark Jackson, or what they simply failed to take into consideration, is how much he worked to make himself better. What they couldn't measure was the size of his heart. He worked at it. He proved that talent alone is not enough. You have to work to make yourself better and nobody worked harder than Mark. He was in the gym every day during the summer after his senior year, getting in shape, working on his shooting, working, working, working to improve. It paid off for him and I couldn't be prouder of him.

Take a kid like Kevin Williams. Here's a kid I just couldn't get through to. A world of talent, but something was missing. He refused to conform. I called his father in when Kevin was a freshman. Ronnie Rutledge was there.

"Mr. Williams," I said, "I can't coach your kid. Get him out of here."

I was almost ready to fire this kid, but the thing that turned it around, he came to me and said, "Coach, I want to play." And the way he said it, the look in his eyes, convinced me that he was ready to conform and he was ready to play. He turned out to be a good kid and a very important player for us.

Then there was Frankie Alagia. They said he was too small, too short. And how about Billy Paultz, the Whopper? Nobody thought he could make it. He was 300 pounds of protoplasm. The only time he got into a high school game was when his team was 30 points ahead or 30 points behind.

He goes to Cameron Junior College, where he's playing

four or five minutes a game. I saw him play that summer and I asked him, "Would you come to St. John's?"

He said yes, so he comes to St. John's and has to sit out a year. When he becomes eligible, he's still playing only a couple of minutes a game. Then in his senior year, he's splitting games with another center, Danny Cornelius. But he starts playing pretty well, averaging 14–15 points a game, 8–9 rebounds a game. Next, he gets drafted by the Virginia Squires mainly because of his size.

I get the job with the Nets and I work a deal to bring him to New York. The first day of practice, September 13, 1970, Rick Barry takes one look at him and says, "Where did you get that big schlub?"

Paultz makes the team as the 12th man—I was picking the squad, not Rick Barry. Midway in the season, our center Eddie Johnson gets hurt and I have to go to the Whopper, Billy Paultz. The big schlub. Not only does he become a good player, he becomes an all-star and he wound up playing fifteen seasons in the NBA. That shows what you can do with hard work and determination, and that's the kind of story that makes you feel good as a coach.

I experienced the ultimate thrill for a coach during the 1984 Olympics in Los Angeles when two of my players competed, Chris Mullin for the United States team, Bill Wennington for the Canadian team. I hadn't planned on attending the Olympics because I had no official function with our basketball team. But the more I thought about Chris and Bill playing in the Games, the more I realized I had to be there.

I called Katha Quinn and asked her to get me a hotel in Los Angeles, I had decided to go out for the Olympics.

"I know it's short notice," I said (it was only a couple of days before the Games were scheduled to start). "Just do the best you can."

Katha calls back and tells me she has a room for me in Los Angeles and I pack and take the next plane out. I check into my hotel and the whole place is filled with Japanese. I was the only American in the joint. If you can imagine this, I was the tallest person in the place. Nobody spoke English. Maybe they thought my name was Carnesaki.

I didn't see any other events, just basketball. I got to see Chris and Bill and my good friend, Antonio Diaz Miguel, the coach of the Spanish team who won the silver medal and who has been one of the leading coaches in Europe over the last 20 years.

Antonio is a frequent visitor to the United States. He'll spend time with Pete Newell, John Wooden and Dean Smith, and he always manages to come to St. John's. When Antonio is here, the talk is all basketball. He has some great ideas about the game and he has given me some excellent hints and suggestions. As a matter of fact, some of the plays we're using now originated from his brain.

I got to visit with the great Hank Iba and Pete Newell, two of the greatest minds the game of basketball has known. It was basketball, basketball, basketball, but it was such a great experience. I enjoyed it immensely. I came back rejuvenated. It gave me a needed shot in the arm to come back and work with more vigor and enthusiasm. Sometimes a thing like that will do that for you.

For two weeks, I overdosed on basketball. I saw every game, thirty-five of them. The only game I didn't see was China against Egypt. I was there, but I fell asleep. Believe me, you would fall asleep, too, watching that game. I think there were the referees, the scorekeepers and me. Nobody else.

I don't think there's a great deal of difference between most coaches in the technical side of the game, just as there isn't a great deal of difference in the talent of most first line players. The difference is in hard work and dedication and motivation.

My way of trying to motivate my players is to tell them how good they can be; to build them up instead of tearing them down. Tearing them down can be counter-productive. I try to put myself in their place. Nobody likes to hear about his faults, especially in public. I can always do that in private. I'm a believer in the old adage that you can attract more bees with honey than you can with vinegar.

If you play for me, I want you to know one thing: I need you more than you need me. That's the way I was taught. That's the way it has always been. That's the way it is now. And that's the way it will always be as long as I continue to coach.

Except for its growth over the last ten years or so and the increased skill of the people who play it, the game of basketball hasn't changed dramatically since Dr. James Naismith and his peach basket. Despite these subtle changes, it still all comes down to basics. The team that puts the ball in the hoop more often, rebounds better, and plays tougher defense is the team that usually will win. And as we head toward the year 2000, I see more gradual changes in the game but nothing truly radical.

To me, the biggest single change in the game in my forty years in basketball has been the size, strength, and skill of the players. Without being too provincial, I think it's fair to say that basketball players are the greatest athletes in the world.

Take Wilt Chamberlain, for example. In my opinion, Wilt probably was the greatest athlete the world has known. Here's a guy seven feet, two inches tall, of enormous strength, and truly remarkable agility. He was a hurdler in college. In his forties, he was a world class volley ball player. He has been a harness racing driver. And he once considered an offer to fight Muhammad Ali for the heavyweight championship of the world. It never came off, which probably is for the best, but I don't think Wilt would have embarrassed himself in the ring.

There are others, like Kareem Abdul-Jabbar, Dr. J, Rick Barry, Oscar Robertson, Elgin Baylor, Magic Johnson, Larry Bird, Patrick Ewing, Michael Jordan. The things these guys could do with their bodies is amazing. There is a beauty about basketball, a certain ballet to it. Is it massive? Is it brutal? Yes, but there's beauty, too, a certain flow, a certain melody unfolds, a certain composition when you see passes and guys flying through the air doing pirouettes. It's pure ballet when you see a Doctor J or a Michael Jordan do what they can do. And it's creative, almost like a great composer at the piano creating new music.

They're the greatest athletes in the world and these are not little people, mind you. I don't think the average person realizes the size and skill of these people. You have only to walk through an airport terminal with a professional basketball team, as I have done, to appreciate their enormous size. At my height, most people seem large, but in the company of a basketball team, I feel like a pygmy.

When I first started in the game, the "big man" on a team was maybe 6-7, 6-8. Joe Lapchick was the big man of his day at 6-5. At 6-10, Harry Boykoff, who played at St. John's in the 1940s and George Mikan of DePaul and later the Minneapolis Lakers, were considered giants in their day. A seven-footer was a freak. Usually, he was gangly and uncoordinated. Today, almost every college team has a seven-footer. Some have two. And just about every team is going to have four or five players in the range of 6-9 and taller.

At 6-8, Magic Johnson would have been the big man on most teams thirty or thirty-five years ago. Today, he is a little man in the pros, a point guard who handles the ball.

Because of diet, vitamins, and the natural process of evolution, people are bigger than ever, and basketball players are no exception. When you think about a Manute Bol, who is seven feet, six inches tall, it makes you wonder how tall the big man will be in the year 2000. Will we have our first eight foot basketball player by then? It wouldn't surprise me the way things are going.

It is because people, including basketball players, keep getting bigger and bigger with each generation; that every few years, somebody will complain that it's getting easier and easier to put the ball in the basket and call for raising the hoop from the present ten feet to twelve feet. Basketball's rulesmakers have resisted the temptation to raise the basket up until now, but I'm not sure how long they will continue to resist these changes. I feel it's inevitable, but not necessarily in my lifetime.

Sooner or later, they're probably just going to have to give in to this undeniable fact of nature. With all the changes that have been made, one thing that hasn't changed has been the dimensions of the court, even though we are now playing with bigger people, taller people, faster people. Now you're putting those ten big guys on the same court they used to put ten little guys five feet, nine inches, and six feet tall. Now these same ten guys are six feet, three inches, to seven feet, three inches, tall and pretty soon somebody is going to realize we're running out of space on the basketball court.

I think they're going to have to enlarge the court. If not the length, then certainly the width, just to fit all those big guys on the floor so they won't be stepping on one another and it won't look like a monster maze to the fans.

As for raising the basket, I wouldn't be in favor of it. I don't think it's necessary. I don't think raising the basket is going to change things that much. How high would you raise it? Twelve feet? Fifteen feet? And what would be the purpose? To eliminate the dunk? I don't like that. I thought it was foolish when they outlawed the dunk in college ball about fifteen years ago.

They put that rule in specifically to legislate against one man, Kareem Abdul-Jabbar. I thought it was a mistake, not to mention being prejudicial to one individual. The dunk adds so much to the game. The fans love it and shouldn't that be the bottom line? Shouldn't we do things to please the people who are paying their way into our arenas? The dunk is great action.

No matter how high you raise the basket, the rules still will favor the big guy over the little guy. No matter how high you raise the basket, little guys will still be able to get up and dunk. Look at our guy, Michael Porter. We list him at six feet tall. He's probably closer to 5-10. But he can jump like a man ten inches taller. One day in practice, I thought he was going to take off, go through the glass, through the roof of the gym and take off into space and never come back. That's how high he can get up.

So I say leave the basket at ten feet. We have already widened the lanes to keep the big guy away from the basket and that's enough. No need to raise the basket.

The three-point play? I think it's good. I always have been in favor of it. A lot of coaches don't like it because it takes the game away from them.

The purists are always preaching, work for the perfect shot. Utopia. And there's nothing wrong with that, but, again, we have to consider the fan. The three-point shot brings excitement to the game. It makes a big man out of a little man. It keeps a team in the game right down to the end. You're down 10, 12 points in the last few minutes, you can still tie the score. You're down by three in the final seconds, you have a chance. I like it.

The 45-second clock is a step in the right direction, but I think we're going to have to bring it down a little. Maybe make it a 30-second clock. Forty-five seconds are too many. If you can't get a shot off in forty-five seconds, there's something wrong with your offense. Again, it's for the fan. It gives them more playing action.

For years, I have campaigned for a red, white, and blue basketball, like we used in the American Basketball Association. Once more, that's for the fans' benefit, because it's easier to see from the cheap seats than the orange-brown ball we're using. Let's make the game more interesting and more appealing to the fans. Give them what they like. Add to their enjoyment, don't detract from it.

If players are bigger, better, stronger, and faster today, on the other hand, I don't think coaching is as thorough, for the simple reason that coaches are involved in too many other things. They have too many responsibilities. But the players get more exposure than ever before. Basketball has become a twelve month sport with trips to Europe in the off season, trips to South America, trips to Africa, with the Olympic Games, the Pan American Games, the World Games, the Big Apple Games, the Empire State Games, the University Games. This is an age of specialization and basketball is no exception.

That's one reason you rarely see two-sport athletes any more. The only ones I can think of offhand are John Elway and Bo Jackson. In the old days, you had plenty of them, like Jackie Robinson, Jackie Jensen, Alvin Dark, Dick Groat, the O'Brien twins, Dave DeBusschere, Gene Conley. Stars in two major sports are rare today because all sports have pretty much become twelve month deals.

One change I would like to see in the future is the makeup of our Olympic team. We lost the Olympic gold medal in basketball only once but that day is coming again. And the reason it's coming is that the game is improving around the world. The players are getting bigger and better, just as they are in the United States. And if we don't watch it, they're going to take over the sport that we invented.

In Europe, professional basketball players are making $200,000 and $300,000 a year and these are the players who are playing in the Olympics.

Why should that be? Why should we compete with our collegians against their pros? I say let's send our best players to the Olympics. Let's send Larry Bird and Michael Jordan and Magic Johnson. Why not?

One reason I have heard, which I think is foolish, is that we're afraid it would tarnish the image of the professional game in the United States if we sent our best pros to the Olympics and they got beat. So what? So we lose. There's nothing wrong with that. At least we'd be losing with our best.

I have told you that I expect you will see a union for college athletes. I also think the day is coming, and not very far off, when college coaches are going to unionize. More and more I see the need for it.

Take two recent cases, Gary Colson at New Mexico and Gordy Chiesa at Providence. Colson averaged twenty-two wins a year for five years, 84 percent of his kids graduated, and they fired him. Why? Because he didn't make the NCAAs. It's not right. Gordy Chiesa was hired in August. They gave him a three-year contract, then seven months later they let him go. It's not right. The coaches need a union to correct these injustices. I don't think the schools have a right to do such things.

Now, I feel very strongly about coaches jumping contracts. If a coach gets fired, the school has to make good on the contract, so why shouldn't the coach compensate the school if he gets a better offer from another school and walks out on his contract? A contract is not unilateral. But some schools are too demanding and they don't give a coach a chance, so I'm convinced a union for coaches is coming. And it's going to come soon.

Another thing I believe you will see in the near future is a world National Basketball Association with teams in the United States competing against teams in Europe and maybe even South America and the Orient, all with a common draft.

What makes this feasible is the Concorde. It wouldn't surprise me if this came to pass in the next fifteen years. My information is that there are people talking about this very thing right now. The reason it can work is the way the game has grown abroad in the last fifteen years. Europe has good players. In fact, teams in the United States are already drafting players from Europe, so it makes sense that there will be expansion of the NBA to Europe. You can fly to Paris and London in three hours. It takes almost six hours to fly from New York to Los Angeles.

Don't misunderstand me. I'm not a great advocate of change. I'm not in favor of change for change sake. We have a great game just the way it is, but it can always be better, especially if we want to continue to appeal to the greatest number of people. If change is necessary, we should do it, provided we don't alter the basic nature of this great game and we never lose sight of the fact that it's the players who are the marquee names—whose unique talent and remarkable skill are what we are selling and are what has made the game of basketball the great game it is.

EIGHTEEN

Looking Ahead

On March 17, 1988, in the Huntsman Center in Salt Lake City, Utah, we were beaten 62–59 by the University of Florida in the second round of the NCAA tournament to put an end to my thirty-eighth year of coaching, including high school, college, professional and as an assistant at St. John's to Joe Lapchick. As soon as that game was over, I began to look ahead to the 1988–1989 season. I started making plans to line up our high school recruits and, in my mind, I was already plotting my roster for the following season.

That's the beauty of sports. There is always another game and another season. For that reason, you never can get too high when you win and you never can get too low when you lose.

In the business we're in, it's now. What you did yesterday doesn't mean a thing. You can't take out your clippings. I can never afford the luxury of thinking I have earned a slide, or an off year, because of what I did in the past. If you do that, you're dead. This is a competitive business and the guy on the other bench, coaching against you, is not going to give you a break because you may have started in the business before he was born or because of your career record. He wants to win just as badly as you do.

Also, you can't afford the luxury of a slide because that wouldn't be fair to your players. Some of them may be seniors, hoping for a professional career, so every game is vital to them. As bad as things may be, you have to be up all the time for the sake of your kids, your fans and your employers.

I suppose, by the way they measure such things, I have had a successful career. If that's the case, I owe that success to a lot of people. I have had some excellent assistant coaches and a great many outstanding players. I have had the good fortune to work at a great university with two great presidents, Father Flynn and Father Cahill, two outstanding athletic directors, Walter McLaughlin and Jack Kaiser, and with excellent athletic moderators, Father Casey, Father Graham, Father Honsberger, Father Keefe, Father Mannion, Father Trainor, Father Kiernan, Father Rivard. And I have had the good fortune to have been in the right place at the right time, a series of events that put me where I am today.

This is not false modesty I'm handing you. I believe those things. But I'm not going to try to snow you. I feel I have had a part in that success. I came to this profession with a good, old-fashioned work ethic that I acquired from my parents. I have put in a lot of hard work and a lot of long hours at great sacrifice to my family. As I have said so often, I would not marry me. I never have been a clock-watcher, but when you love what you do, you don't watch the clock and you don't count the hours.

Make no mistake, I love the thing that I do. I love every minute of it. I never felt like it was a job. I felt it has been more of a hobby. I think I have brought a great dedication and determination on my part. I put all my efforts into it. Everything. It has been my whole life.

And I think our philosophy here at St. John's has been an important contributor to that success. A professionalism going all the way back to Buck Freeman, one of the greatest coaches of all-time who coached one of the greatest teams of all-time, the Wonder Five. If they had a lead, you wouldn't see the ball for six months. Buck established the theory that you should do just a few things, but do them well. Whatever you do, do it well. If you go to a clinic, do it well. Keep it simple.

Why change that philosophy? If you win three out of every four games, why change it completely? Just for the sake of changing? Stay with what has been successful. If pressing defense is the key, then why don't the teams that press win all the time? It's because it's what you do at the other end that counts. Do you convert?

A few years ago, coach Judd Heathcote's Michigan team won the national championship with a match-up zone. How come he didn't win every year? You know why? Because the year he won, he had Magic Johnson. The great St. Bonaventure team with the Stith Brothers, Tom and Sam, won with a pressing defense. How come they didn't win when those guys were gone? Because those guys converted at the other end.

Defense helps you win, no question about it. If two teams are equal, then defense will win. But it's not the bottom line. It's the players that convert it at the other end that make you win. They talk about the fast break. When you get down to the final analysis, in big games, there aren't too many fast breaks because everything is measured. Everything becomes magnified. Every play becomes important. The scores aren't 130–125 in big games. Go back and look at the great series between the Knickerbockers and the Lakers, Boston and Milwaukee, Boston and the Lakers. The scores aren't haywire. Maybe once in awhile. The scores are low because everything is measured. Fast break teams, pressing defenses will win occasionally. But why don't they win all the time? Because it's got to be a combination, offense and defense.

Our philosophy is take good care of the ball. If the ball is valuable, don't give it up that easily. Don't treat it carelessly.

The St. John's philosophy is the philosophy of the Vincentian Fathers who founded the university. It's a Thomistic philosophy, as espoused by St. Thomas Aquinas. *Vitus et medias stat.* Somewhere in the middle of the road. A combination of offense and defense. That balance. The influence of the Vincentian Fathers, which is a family situation. They influenced us as coaches and they did it low key because they work with the poor. That's their basic philosophy and it rubs off on all of us.

Father Flynn, then the president of St. John's, set the tone at the press conference to dedicate the opening of Alumni Hall. It was in 1962, right after the basketball scandal. Everybody thought we were going to deemphasize, but Father Flynn came in and said we're going to reemphasize.

"Just because there's a little dirt in the corner," Father Flynn said, "you don't knock down the whole building."

Then he issued a warning to the coaches.

"Cheat and you're fired."

And that set the tone that still prevails today.

To me the big thing is how am I going to end all this. Or will I have it ended for me? St. John's no longer has the mandatory retirement at age sixty-five that forced Joe Lapchick to retire while he was still in his prime as a coach, so there is no timetable that is staring me in the face. I know it has to end sometime and I may not even have any control over it.

I know there is always the temptation to want one more year or one more recruiting class. The problem with that is if you recruit a class, you want to see that class through to the end, but by the time that class is in its senior year, you have already recruited another class and you have more or less made a commitment to those kids that you will be there. So, you can see it's a never-ending merry-go-round.

Anything can happen. I don't have a scenario about my retirement because I don't think about it that much. I don't know if I can think about retirement. How do you walk away after all these years of doing something you always wanted to do, something you love, and something that still excites you? I know this. I don't want to die with my boots on. I don't want to be like a fighter who wants just one more fight. When it's time to go, I just want to go. Enough. That's it. And it will have nothing to do with wins or losses.

A lot of people, well-meaning people, say it would be great if I could win a national title and then walk away. Believe me, winning a national championship has never been a big thing for me. Sure, it would be nice, for me, the kids and for the university, but I don't feel that would be the culmination of my coaching career or the final point.

I want to play it day by day. I'm not going to put a date on my retirement because I have no control over it. I'm not going to make any plans. I never make plans. I've never said I want to do this or do that. Everything that has happened to me, just happened. Right now, I'm having too much fun coaching. I'm still involved, I still care about winning and losing, and my mind is still too active. As long as I feel the way I do now, I'll continue to coach, if St. John's will continue to have me.

Sometimes you look at your job and you say, "I'd rather be doing something else." I'm fortunate that I never said that, but it can happen and I'm reminded of a poignant scene I witnessed involving the former governor of New York, Hugh Carey, another St. John's man. I first met him when I was coaching high school and he was a congressman and we got to know each other. After he became Governor, I was giving a clinic one time at a state fair in Syracuse.

Governor Carey showed up and he said to me, "Lou, why don't you fly home with me?"

I accepted and we flew down to LaGuardia Airport in his private plane. On the way down, he said, "I'm so tired of this. I have people pushing me here, pulling me there. Do this. Do that."

It struck me what a lonely man he was. But there was a very human side of him. When we arrived at the airport, his daughter and his grandsons were waiting for him. They greeted him warmly, with hugs and kisses, as if they hadn't seen him in some time. That was a moving thing to see. And I thought about it for a long time. Here was the top man in the state and he had no peace, no quiet. And he was so happy to see his family. That impressed me very much. He was the number one man in the state, but he couldn't wait to leave public life and go into private life.

If the time ever comes that I no longer enjoy coaching, no longer find it challenging and fun, or that it just gets to be too much for me, that's when I'll step down. That hasn't happened yet. But, as I say, the decision to step down may be made for me. If the university thinks it would be better off going in another direction, maybe put a younger man in the job, I'll accept their decision with no bitterness and no regrets.

If and when the time comes that I am no longer coaching, I have some things I'd like to consider doing with the rest of my life. One thing I don't want to do is retire and do nothing. I just couldn't be inactive. I'm pretty sure I'll remain involved on the international scene. I'd like to keep my hand in the game in some way and I'd always like to be involved in coaching. I can be a consultant, I can do clinics here and overseas. I like to teach. I love teaching.

Basically, I'm a teacher and I can see myself in the role of a teacher.

Another thing I don't want to do is look over somebody else's shoulder. Joe Lapchick told me that many years ago. Buck Freeman didn't do it. Lapchick didn't do it. And I won't do it. I'll make certain I'm not in the building, not hanging around, unless my successor is the type of individual who would want me around because he thinks I can help. Then I'll help him in any way I can.

I know it can't go on forever. I'm not looking forward to the day it ends, but I'm not afraid of it, either.

When it does happen, I'll walk away without any regrets. Hey, I consider myself very fortunate. I did what I always wanted to do and it's the only job I ever had. I made enough money to take care of my family. I got a measure of recognition. I had the pleasure of coaching some great players and great kids. I worked for excellent people at a great institution and I never had to punch a clock. And I made some wonderful friends, not only in this country, but around the world.

In return, I hope I have given something back to the game. I hope I have given our fans some pleasure, that I have represented my school well and that I helped mold some young people into good, upstanding citizens.

I have had a ball. I would never have made a good doctor and there's just so much salami you can slice.